BATTLES: GLIMPSES OF TRUTH

Stories and Poems

Dot Day and Barbara Gaddy

Copyright 2024 © Dorothy A. Day and Barbara G. Gaddy

All rights reserved

Printed in the United States of America

No parts of this book may be used or reproduced in any form or manner without written permission, except in the case of reviews.

Battles: Glimpses of Truth / Dot Day and Barbara Gaddy

Cover Design by: Barbara Gaddy, Dot Day, and Genesis Publishing House

ISBN (Paperback): 979-8-9905012-8-7
ISBN (Hardcover): 979-8-9905012-9-4
ISBN (eBook): 979-8-9905012-7-0

DEDICATION

Battles: Glimpses of Truth is dedicated to those who currently have and those who have had struggles and battles in their lives.

"If you're going through hell, keep going."

Winston Churchill

"Life is 10% what happens to you and 90% how you react to it."

Charles R. Swindoll

A portion of the profits from the sale of ***Battles: Glimpses of Truth*** will go to support two worthy organizations – Forever Homes and VHPA Scholarships.

Forever Homes

There is a pressing need for homes and day services in Mississippi for individuals with intellectual and developmental disorders, including those with autism spectrum disorder. A group of concerned family members and friends formed an organization, Raising Forever Homes, to solicit funds to build and maintain homes to provide the care needed on a 24-hour-7-day-a-week basis.

Their dreams include residences and farmsteads, a community center with gardens for vegetables and flowers, a barnyard, barns, and pasture for domesticated animals.

For their young adults who have aged out of the school setting, the Raising Forever Homes organization envisions "a forever home where they can experience life to the fullest and grow old."

VHPA – Vietnam Helicopter Pilots Association Scholarships

The Vietnam Helicopter Pilots Association (administered by AAAA – the Army Aviation Association of America) provides scholarships for descendants of Vietnam veterans. All VHPA scholarships are open only to the descendants of VHPA members in good standing currently or at their death. By providing these scholarships to the descendants of Vietnam Veterans, the VHPA and AAAA continue to honor those who valiantly served America – both those who returned, and those who gave their all on the battlefield. For more information on applying for these scholarships, visit https://www.vhpa.org/vhpa_scholarship.htm.

Glimpses of Truth

Dot Day

Home are the prisoners
Tending their loss.
Home is the doctor
After carrying his cross.
Home is the survivor
Escaping the charge.
Home is the pilot
Grounded by time.
Home is the soldier
Lamenting his loss.
Home is the swimmer
Katrina's memory deep remnant gone.
Home is the mother
Tending the shrine.

Stories of success, survival, making a difference despite pain and loss – these are the tales and poems of ordinary people who battled. Some still do.

TABLE OF CONTENTS

20/20 Determination 1
Barbara Gaddy

The Twenty-Fourth of May...9
Lottie Brent Boggan

Seventy-Five Years, Come and Gone 13
Lottie Brent Boggan

I Am 17
Gail Harvey-Walker

War Diary of Staff Sgt. Hardin M. Wright....................19
Staff Sgt. Hardin M. Wright

Coaching to Win 45
Dot Day

Medical Missions...49
Philip Levin, M.D

Swimming Katrina – or Black Lace and Broken Sandals............63
Barbara Gaddy

Bruce Gaddy: Death Dealer #22 –
"Nineteen Minutes to Live" 73
Bruce Gaddy as told to Dot Day and Barbara Gaddy

Maudie 91
Dr. Bob Rich

Commercials, TV & Old Age 99
Hazel Lonie

Awakening to God's Love...101
Cindy Mount

TopGun: Steve Spragg's Story....................................105
Dot Day

To John Upon His Return 113
Carol Ashley

Stoic Patriot Bill Day 115
Dot Day

Black Water 143
Gail Harvey-Walker

Introverted Excellence 145
Barbara Gaddy

Is God Good? 155
Patti Lamar

Naked on the Back Porch..159
Dot Day

Vagabond..163
Gail Shows Bouldin

I Have Met the Enemy 167
Cindy Mount

To my Son, Archie Ray Bush. Jr., 1972-2009............................171
Lynn Bush King

Zeb, Gunner, and Kye..177
Barbara Gaddy

Nothing in Life Is Free..195
Janet Taylor Perry

The Swordsman 199
Gail Harvey-Walker

The Ground Forces 201
Dot Day

Cucumbers and Pickles – My Story of Battling PTSD..............205
Josh Dawson

A Tall Glass of Tell-It-Like-It-Is Juice........................213
David Ching

From Boredom to Brilliance 223
Barbara Gaddy

Drought 229
Dot Day

Sweet Relief..231
Pauline Rule

Memorial Day with Granny 241
Jas Clark

Two Freds – 2023...245
Fred Crans

War Effort...253
Lottie Brent Boggan

About the Authors...259

Contributors 263

20/20 DETERMINATION
Barbara Gaddy

My first-born, Patrick Taylor, loves airplanes.
As a young boy, he built model planes – all types – and we hung them from the ceiling with fishing line. His bedroom looked like a mini aviation museum.

His love of all things airplanes was encouraged by his grandfather – my father Ray Grillot – who also loved airplanes and flying. Ray-Ray as he was affectionately known, took Patrick to his Army Air Corps Squadron reunions where Patrick would wear his grandfather's military jacket. The squadron buddies loved that, loved Patrick, and made him feel oh-so-special. Ray-Ray also took my two sons, Patrick and Daniel, with him on flights in a small Cessna – and would buzz our house in Crystal Springs, Mississippi, with all of the rest of the family standing in the front yard waving as they buzzed us. Patrick later proved his aviation excellence and that "specialness" in the air.

Me, his mom? Well, I knew he enjoyed the models and loved attending the squadron reunions with my dad. But I had no idea of what was to come in Patrick's future or the determination and drive my son had to make his dream of being a Navy jet pilot come true!

Fast-forward to Patrick's college days. He was attending Louisiana State University (LSU) in Baton Rouge, Louisiana, and was working in the flooring department at the local Lowe's to help pay his way through college. I'll never forget getting a phone call from Patrick one night and hearing, "Mom, I've quit my job." And my typical mom response was to ask, "Why? What are you doing that for? How are you going to help pay for college?" And probably some other questions. I will also never forget his response to me verbatim: "Mom, I'd rather pump shit out of planes and be around them than not to be around them at all."

And thus began his life of "being around planes – actual planes." He began at the far outskirts of the Baton Rouge airport, visiting every private plane facility, hangar, company, asking if he could get a job with them – doing anything – just to be able to "be around airplanes."

Executive Aviation hired him – to "pump the shit" out of the private planes and other chartered planes that used their facility. He cleaned the planes upon landing, refueled them, and got them ready for their return flights. During that time, he enjoyed meeting many celebrities who were flying in for events. While working there, Patrick also took advantage of being able to take private pilot lessons.

Easy entry into Naval aviation, you may think. Not really. You see, Patrick had corrected vision – and military pilots are not approved for flight training if they have corrected vision. Here's the point where the story gets really good.

While still a student at LSU, (and unbeknownst to his mother), Patrick was making regular trips to Houston, Texas, and talking with Navy recruiters about his dreams of becoming a Navy pilot. And not just "any pilot." A *jet* pilot. He still had the corrected vision issue to confront, and the recruiters told him straight out that he could not qualify to be a pilot with corrected vision.

Not to be deterred, Patrick continued his visits to meet with his recruiter and completed all the flight tests, including written tests

Battles: Glimpses of Truth

and simulation tests, scoring in the highest percentage on all the flight requirement tests.

His vision? Well, he did his research and learned that the Navy was considering – only *considering* – waiving the vision requirements if the recruit's vision was corrected via PRK surgery. "What's that?" you ask. Photorefractive keratectomy (PRK) is a type of refractive surgery. This kind of surgery uses a laser to treat vision problems caused by refractive errors. You have a refractive error when your eye does not refract (bend) light properly. With PRK, your ophthalmologist uses a laser to change the shape of your cornea. This improves the way light rays are focused on the retina. PRK is used to treat myopia (nearsightedness), hyperopia (farsightedness) and astigmatism.

So, is that the same as LASIK? Nope. So if LASIK and PRK are both a form of laser corneal surgery, what exactly makes them different from one another? The basic difference is that PRK requires the surgeon to remove the surface cells of the cornea. Recovery time is longer than with LASIK. And, the key difference for Patrick was that PRK was the *only* vision corrective surgery being considered for waiver for Navy aviators.

Ok, enough technical medical stuff.

Patrick saved his money, had the PRK surgery, and his vision was corrected to better than 20/20. So – on to Navy flight school, right? Not so fast. Remember the Navy was still just *considering* PRK vision correction for their approved waiver. Following his successful surgery, the recruiter reminded Patrick of that fact. And Patrick's reply? "Well, if I didn't have the PRK, I knew I'd never be able to fly. This way, I'll at least be ready if they waive the requirement."

Patrick was set to graduate from LSU in May 2002. In October 2001, Patrick had called his recruiter to ask if the events following September 11, 2001, and the invasion of Afghanistan were going to delay his application. In November 2001, the recruiter called

Dot Day and Barbara Gaddy

Patrick at work one evening, and asked him if he was sitting down, – and informed him that the Navy had just waived the corrected vision requirement if the correction was done using PRK. Patrick was ready!

In June 2002, Patrick went to Officer Candidate School (OCS) at Naval Station Pensacola, Florida, where he received his commission in the United States Navy. Following that initial training at OCS, he also received his longed-for dream assignment to train as a pilot.

His training took him to Naval Air Station Meridian, Mississippi, where he received his wings. While there he treated me to a "flight" in a T-45 training jet simulator, with me as the pilot since most jets are single-seat, and him outside the simulator on the headset intercom with me. Wow! What a realistic experience. I gained even more appreciation for jet pilots through this experience.

Some of his following assignments and locations took him to Corpus Christi, Texas; Lemoore, California; Iwakuni, Japan; Fallon, Nevada; and Virginia Beach, Virginia.

But, let me tell you about his aircraft carrier landing qualifications. He, along with his squadron, readied their jets and headed from their base to an aircraft carrier in the Pacific to perform their qualifying aircraft carrier landings. Prior to departing for the carrier, Patrick's jet developed mechanical difficulties, and he was forced to remain behind for the necessary repairs. The mechanical adjustments took longer than anticipated, requiring him to stay overnight – which meant that the next day, as a young jet pilot, he had to make his way alone to "locate" the carrier in the Pacific Ocean. That task completed, of course, the next task was landing on that carrier, which he did successfully. His squadron buddies had, by the time Patrick joined them on the carrier, completed their required number of maneuvers – with touch-and go's – wave-off's – completed take-off's and landings. It was nearing nightfall when Patrick arrived at the carrier, the weather conditions were

Battles: Glimpses of Truth

worsening, and visibility levels were quickly lowering. Patrick was told that if he was going to perform his qualifying landings, he would need to complete ALL his required landings immediately – *that night* – with the rolling waves, strong winds, and low visibility – otherwise, he would have to wait for the next scheduled carrier quals, six weeks away.

You are probably ahead of me here – Patrick's 20/20 determination kicked in – and under difficult conditions and added pressure, he successfully completed his qualifications. When he later called me to tell me he had qualified on his carrier landings, his comment was, "It wasn't pretty, but I qualified." Even his squadron buddies told him they didn't know how he did it. When Patrick completed his landings, the ship immediately headed back to port. I remember telling him that he was being prepared for possible difficult future landings – and that his squadron mates didn't have the benefit of that difficult experience he had that night. I believe he was being prepared for some future real-life challenges and experiences.

One of the discussions he and I had has remained with me in a special way, though many are very memorable. During one conversation he was telling me about some particularly treacherous activities he had. When I replied with a chuckle, "Son, your mom doesn't need to know all of the things that you do," he quickly responded with, "Yes, mom, you do need to know." And I took the bait and asked him, "Ok, tell me why!" I'll remember his words forever – "Because it means I'm good enough to bring my squadron home safely." Yes, I really did need to know that! And that security of knowledge in his skill, his dedication, and his confidence carried me many times when he was flying missions to "who knows where."

Now, on with the story. You know what's located in Fallon, Nevada, right? Yep – TopGun – NSAWC – the Naval Strike Air Warfare Center. While there, Patrick attended the TopGun Adversary Pilot course, helping to train young jet pilots in the classroom as well as in the air – participating in air-to-air combat training in the VFC-13 "Saints" Adversary Squadron – being the *adversary* against those young pilots he trained – hoping they would be better than he in the dogfights and at the same time trying not to let them do that very thing. What a perspective for an instructor!

When I was planning a visit to Fallon to see him, he called to ask me if I still had my security clearance from my place of employment. My first thought was *Do I have to have a clearance to go visit my son?* I told him, "Yes, I have my Top Secret clearance." His next comment was incredible to me. He said, "Well, I was just thinking. I can't tell anyone else in the family what I really do. But since you have a clearance, would you like to go to work with me one day while you are here? I can get you cleared for that if you want to." *If I want to? I was ecstatic!*

The day I went to "work" with my child was phenomenal – and memorable – and included a couple of interesting and perhaps light-hearted moments. As we were checking in to the NSAWC facility, one of his buddies walked past us in the lobby, looked at Patrick and me, and simply said, "Dude …" and then just continued walking into the facility. Patrick gave him a slight smile and nod. I was concerned that Patrick was getting teased about "bringing his mom to work." But his response floored me. "No, they just think it's so cool that I have a mom who has this clearance!"

The day was filled with enlightening and fascinating moments and briefings. But, of course, I can't share those! As we were winding down the day, we were in a room filled with young military personnel performing various duties, when a young man hurriedly came over to us and said, "Sir, she needs to leave." Patrick very calmly explained that I had proper clearance (it was indicated on my badge as well), but the young man insisted that I leave. Not to cause a disturbance, we exited the room and were walking down the hallway to the exit when the commander of the facility came hurrying out to catch up to us. He was apologizing for the young pilot's actions in asking me to leave, telling me that I had a higher clearance than anyone there!! My honest reaction, and my comment to him, was, "I understand completely. You don't need to apologize. I truly appreciate that he was taking his job seriously and protecting the facility, the information, and all involved." He graciously thanked me for my understanding and invited me back at any time. And we left after a day full of fabulous experiences and memories.

Remember the flights with Ray-Ray that he had as a young boy? Buzzing our house? Well, on one visit to Virginia Beach, Patrick became that pilot, taking his mom up in a small two-seater private plane. We flew along the beautiful Atlantic coastline for hours, with my son as my pilot and guide. I've been blessed with so many shared experiences throughout his pilot journey.

Patrick has had many more assignments. One of his most recent was as the Commanding Officer of the VR-62 "Nomads" C-130 squadron stationed at Naval Air Station, Jacksonville, Florida. I was fortunate to attend the Change of Command ceremony when he received his orders to become the CO.

He gave me his coffee mug imprinted with the patch from his first squadron in Lemoore, California, and his first "call sign" – where it all began. No, it really didn't begin there – his dream actually began as a young boy building airplane models, flying with his RayRay, and dreaming of one day being a jet pilot.

"Patrick, you can't be accepted into Navy flight school with corrected vision," he was told by the Navy recruiter many years ago. And, at the time, that was true.

Little did they know that Patrick had **20/20 Determination** – which led to 20/20 vision, a career as an F-18 Navy fighter pilot, a TopGun instructor, and a Commanding Officer among his other assignments, some of which I will never know.

THE TWENTY-FOURTH OF MAY

Lottie Brent Boggan

May 24, 2020

Many people in this great country of ours are helping others now, in so many ways.

Despite so much uncertainty and with our lives indefinitely upended since the beginning of the corona virus pandemic, people and communities are coming together to support one another during this world crisis. Right now, untold numbers of nurses and doctors are busy fighting for our lives and risking theirs, as are others: grocery store workers, policeman, truck drivers, firefighters, sanitation workers, too many to name. But, they're out there. And, aren't we grateful and proud?

We appreciate the heroes. There always have been, and there always will be, those who should earn our gratitude

Car doors slamming outside break my reverie and I check my watch; eleven o'clock. "Okay. If everybody's here, we're right on time," I say.

For many years, on this day, May 24, I have been compelled – no, driven – to go to the cemetery and to pay homage to my husband's younger brother, Second Lieutenant Robert Thomas

Boggan. This year I will have company. This is our first family gathering since the corona virus pandemic; we plan to honor our hero today.

On the drive to Lakewood Cemetery and because of today's date and where we're going, I think back to another time. Long before there was this pandemic there were those who have endured, not a medical pandemic, but a different kind of world crisis: World War II – where 70 to 85 million lives were lost – those numbers so staggering I can't take them in.

May 24, 1945

World War II, and copilot Bobby Boggan was on his seventh mission. The pilots who flew the B-29s to Japan and back had as rigorous – if not the most dangerous – duty of any combat crew in World War II. For the eleven men in each super fortress, the fifteen-hour flights were an eternity of tension, broken by moments of mortal danger.

That night, on a low-level bombing run, a strike force of 520 planes dropped 3,646 tons of incendiary, targeting the Kamikaze factories in Japan. The weather was poor, the target area almost entirely obscured by low clouds, probing searchlights, blinding smoke, and heavy flak.

Frequently hidden from the B-29 gunners by the glare of searchlights, Japanese night fighters dove in from every quarter; thousands of guns blasted the sky. The Raiders lost seventeen planes that night. Bobby's plane was hit. The B-29, badly damaged, its crew was ordered to bail.

The crewmen were able to parachute out; they saw the plane crash. Then they were captured. But the bombardier, navigator, pilot, and copilot Bobby Boggan had to crawl through a metal tube to reach the bomb bay doors before they could parachute to safety.

Battles: Glimpses of Truth

They didn't make it. The four of them went down with their plane on May 24, 1945.

Bobby's remains lay buried deep in foreign soil. A friend of the family went to Japan shortly after the war and spent much of her time visiting cemeteries, looking for Robert Thomas Boggan, Clinton, Mississippi. She found where they had laid him. His body was sent to Memphis, where the Boggans had an old family burial plot.

He lay there for years but was still not home.

"We want him closer. Will you help us?" his mother asked me. I said I would.

Willard and his family felt it was best for them not to know the time or the date. It was my honor and privilege to make the arrangements, and some months later I got word that his remains would be sent from Memphis.

May 24, 1964

Exactly nineteen years to the day since Bobby Boggan had been killed, a preacher, my Big Mama, and I went to Lakewood Cemetery.

The coffin was rusty, bits of old dirt clinging to it, but it was iron and intact.

The three of us had scripture and a prayer; I tried not to cry as an American hero was laid to rest. There was no twenty-one-gun salute, no planes flying overhead in a fallen comrade formation. His funeral congregation were men standing with their shovels.

My heart aching, I turned to walk away, but felt there needed to be something more and ran back.

"Wait a minute," I called to one of the nearby men leaning on his shovel. I bent over, kissed the rusty coffin, and whispered, "That's from me and the rest of the family."

The man answered in a soft voice. "Mr. Bobby and I used to play together. I found out he was coming home. I asked to help dig his grave."

Tears flowing, he and I hugged each other.

Bobby was home.

"We live in fame, go down in flame."

Seventy-five years ago today, Bobby Boggan was shot down.

It will be his family's privilege to place a flag over and say a prayer of thanks for Second Lieutenant Robert Thomas Boggan who gave his life for our country and for the world.

God bless America!

And an expression I've often heard came to mind, "As long as there's someone alive to tell their story, a person does not die."

Let us not forget!

SEVENTY-FIVE YEARS, COME AND GONE

Lottie Brent Boggan

May 24, 2020

As I have done for many years, on May 24, the date Second Lieutenant Robert Thomas Boggan's B-20 bomber was shot down in 1945, I am at Lakewood Cemetery. There is one big difference about today's visit though; I am not alone; I have collateral descendants of Bobby Boggan with me, each carrying an American flag and flowers to put on our fallen warrior's grave.

Tomorrow is Memorial Day and I am in the car with son Bill, daughter-in-law Binnie Jo, and granddaughter Peyton Boggan. As we drive on through the cemetery, it makes me feel good when I notice there are many American flags out on this Sunday. As usual, I am humbled by what so many heroic people have meant, not only to our country, but to the world as we know and live in it today.

Sometimes we forget that the freedoms we now enjoy were purchased with the blood of our fallen patriots, "Who more than self, their country loved." There have been other conflicts, but World War II was the worst in human history. I thank God that miraculously the body of Willard's brother made it home.

Dot Day and Barbara Gaddy

I'm sure age has a lot to do with it, but to me that generation of soldiers and the people back home are unforgettable. With the vast majority of those veterans past the age of ninety, it won't be long before only a few will be left to tell their stories of courage and triumph in the face of overwhelming odds.

Eight years old when Pearl Harbor was bombed, I would fill up pages if I named the stars and celebrities who were in that conflict and what they did, so I'll limit myself to five still recognizable names: James Stewart, Paul Newman, Tony Curtis, Charlton Heston, Robert Stack (I danced with him.).

Those years made quiet heroes out of countless soldiers, scientists, teachers, cooks, students, farm workers. Whether they were fighting the Nazis on the European front or making a difference against the Japanese in the Pacific, these down-to-earth people helped lead the Allies to victory and make the world what it is today.

Time marches on and sadly memories of World War II and those selfless persons are fading from our minds; they no longer make headlines, but many of my generation are still humbled by what those heroes meant, not only to our country, but to the world as we know and live in it today.

Those of us who were children during those years were not of the greatest generation; but because of the world situation and because of being reared by them, discipline and honesty were a way of life at home and at school. We were not allowed to be pampered and spoiled.

I don't think, even if they had been around, we would have been addicted to today's distractions: televisions, computers, cell phones, video games. Now, please try to hear me and understand; I do realize that I am out of the loop in so many ways.

I'm also sure that this is an age thing, and I'll probably have wet noodles thrown at me for bringing this up, but in the past few years I have believed that sometimes too many Americans may pay homage to the wrong persons. I'm thinking about athletes, actors, and rap stars.

Looking back through recent times, before Covid-19, it was kinda hard for me to come up with some names; but in this day and age, with the pandemic virus, that seems to have turned around somewhat. Celebrities today can't fly war planes or drive tanks; and like the rest of the world, they have had to isolate. But many of them are stepping up. They are providing food and medical supplies to those who are hungry or sick and donating money where it's needed. Yes, they are out there.

Our car pulls to a stop as does the car behind us.

Today, May 24, 2020, seventy-five years to the day that Bobby Boggan's plane was shot down, some of his collateral descendants and their family members have gathered at Lakewood Cemetery to honor one soldier who gave his life for this country and for the world.

Lottie Brent Boggan – sister-in-law; Bill Boggan – nephew; Bryan Boggan – great nephew; Christian Boggan – great nephew; Peyton Boggan – great-great niece; and Wyatt Boggan – great-great-great nephew. Other loved ones with us on this day are Binnie Jo and Baylee Boggan.

There are some who could not make it – Michelle Ayers, Carter Ayers, Aden Ayers, Trace Kindred, Kyle Kindred.

Those there today saw a picture of Bobby Boggan, then I gave each person a copy of the Air Force song. We all placed a flag on the grave; then son Bill led us in prayer.

The prayer over, I take a deep breath. "You made it home, Bobby Boggan. Rest in peace," I say as we turn away.

And it seems as if I heard a faint voice drifting over the waving flags, granite, brass name markers, and sloping green fields.

"Off we go into the wild blue yonder,
Climbing high into the sun."

I AM

Gail Harvey Walker

I am the nightmare that haunts your dreams,
filling your night with terror and screams.
If you ignore me, you think I will just go away,
but I'll still be a part of your every day.

I am the reason you can't get along,
why you feel like you are always wrong.
When you're mad and looking for a fight,
I'm right there with you, never out of sight.

I am all sadness, guilt, shame, and grief;
I will never give you any relief.
I am every tear your eyes have cried,
why you never even tried.

I am your burden, the anchor of pain,
wrapped around you with an old rusty chain.
I am always pulling you farther down,
making you wonder if you're going to drown.

Dot Day and Barbara Gaddy

I am the monster that hides in the dark,
I keep you away from God's healing spark.
If you would only open the door,
I would be able to exist no more.

06/10/2006

WAR DIARY OF STAFF SGT. HARDIN M. WRIGHT

Staff Sgt. Hardin M. Wright

Hardin McGee Wright (1921-2006), son of Weldon Earl and Donia Gregory Wright, was born April 19, 1921. H. M., as he was called by his family and friends, was the youngest of nine children. His parents moved from Mayfield, Kentucky, in 1916 and purchased land and a two-story log house six miles west of Raymond on Old Port Gibson Road. The log house had been built in 1823. In 1863, on May 11, Colonel Kennedy and Yankee troops camped on the home place. On May 12, the Battle of Raymond began, and on May 13, the troops moved to Jackson and in seven days won three battles, including Jackson and Champion Hill.

In 1865, Kennedy returned from Pennsylvania and bought the house and farm. This is the same house and farm bought by the Weldon Earl Wrights in 1916. In 1920, four rooms were added, sealed inside and outside with drop siding. All of H. M.'s boyhood years were spent on the home place.

H. M. graduated from Union Church in 1938 and then spent two years at Hinds Junior College in Raymond, Mississippi. He took a defense job in Biloxi at Keesler Air Force Base and was a truck driver. He also took civilian pilot's training and got a

Dot Day and Barbara Gaddy

pilot's license. From Biloxi, he went to Camp McCain in Grenada, Mississippi, as a rodman, tying steel. He enlisted May 22, 1942, and was called to active duty in August of 1942, as Aviation Cadet, U.S. Army Air Force, Bombardment Squadron, 99th Bombardment Group APO 520.

Diary of H. M. Wright

We reported to Nashville, Tennessee, and then went on to Montgomery, Alabama, Maxwell Field for pre-flight training. We went to Lakeland, Florida, for primary flight training, then basic flight training in Sumter, South Carolina, and advanced flight training at Spence Field in Moultrie, Georgia. From there we went to Denver, Colorado, where I was joined by Syble Sweeney, my fiancée. We were married on June 29, 1943. Our families lived two and one-half miles apart on Old Port Gibson Road, and I had known her since I was in the eighth grade.

From Denver, the bomber group of ten went to Salt Lake City, Utah, to fly B-17 heavy bombers. The next stop was Alexandria, Louisiana, to fly mock missions, and it was on to Grand Isle, Nebraska, to pick up a brand-new B-17 four-engine bomber equipped with radar. We went to Newport News, Virginia, Langley Field, to fly more mock missions.

My Service Overseas in the European Theater of Operations
By Hardin M. Wright

This account was written by him on scraps and pieces of paper.

May 5th, 1944: At 5:00 a. m., the ring of the alarm clock awakens me to the realization that I have long-awaited duties and must leave my wife for an overseas post to combat the enemy of my country.

Battles: Glimpses of Truth

The first of many hard tasks confronts me in the form of telling my wife goodbye and leaving her. This done, I rush out to catch the bus to the airport.

We board a new 17 G, shiny aluminum B-17 free of paint, representing $300,000 of Uncle Sam's money. Including the radar equipment aboard, the value is far above this figure.

After having loaded our personal and combat equipment, we take off for Morrison Field, West Palm Beach, Florida. On reaching there, we are met [by someone] in a station wagon and carried to the operation building.

We process and have a physical check, then go to our barracks. After two days' preparation we take off on a nonstop flight, 1,750 miles to Trinidad. Upon landing there, we are met by [someone in] a truck and carried to our quarters.

We are greeted with atabrine and a solution to rub on our bodies to prevent mosquito bites. Our beds are under mosquito bars for added protection. We are fed well and briefed for our next stop, which is Belem, Brazil.

The briefing consists of weather reports, field location, and the approximate vicinity of crashed planes along the route. We [are] instructed to look for these planes with high-powered glasses.

May 9th: We go to our plane early and tear up a starter on the number two engine. We are held over for a day or so and go up into the mountains to a large hole under a waterfall, where we enjoy a nice cool swim. After the swim we take a hike through the jungle hunting wild fruits and marveling at the oddities. The following morning our plane is ready, and we take off for Belem. Flying just over the treetops and scanning the countryside for crashed planes [prove] to be futile.

At Belem quarters our mosquito war continues as it does throughout the trip and during our stay in Italy. At Belem we are fed all the fresh pineapple, oranges, and bananas we can eat.

The natives are very dirty and small in stature. They speak Portuguese and are of a color between that of an average American Indian and American black.

Fortaleza, our next stop, is very similar to Belem. We give our plane a thorough check and rest up until the following night at midnight. We hire natives to launder our clothes, keep the tent clean, make beds, and do other odd jobs for fifty cents.

At midnight we take off on a 2,000-mile hop to Dakar, Africa. Shortly after we are out at sea, we strike a storm and climb in an attempt to get over the top (above the clouds). We can't get above the clouds, so we suffer the storm. Lightning flashes seem to set the ship ablaze. Our plane is tossed and beaten by the tough air accompanying the storm. After two hours we get out of the storm but are still under an overcast sky and can't get shots on stars for navigational aid.

At 8:30 a.m. we found out where we are. We have drifted 500 miles north of our course, six hundred miles from shore. We have an estimated four-and-one-half hours gas left, thanks to having flown on automatic lean, not automatic rich. Everyone becomes tense with the realization that we have no gas to spare, if even enough.

The Cape Verde Islands are our first sight of land. They are only rocky cliffs, of no use to us. Finally, we sight the coast of Africa, after thirteen hours and fifteen minutes of flying under our belts.

Dakar's airfield is a dustbowl and desert, with steel mat runways. Surrounding the base are a number of gnarled old trees, hundreds of years old, with trunks up to fifteen feet in diameter and only thirty-to-thirty-five feet in height, including their few small branches.

The natives are jet black with an appearance just as seen in *National Geographic* magazine. Their clothing consists of white dresses without sleeves or collars. The hemline is much higher on the sides than in the front and back. Their eyes, features, and actions remind me more of a wild animal than a human being.

After one night's rest, we take off again. Our next stop is Marrakech, an old French Foreign Legion post, surrounded by olive groves, which are irrigated by an immense hand-dug reservoir. A large number of Italian prisoners are held in the camp. Part of these are prisoners of the French and part prisoners of the U.S. Our prisoners receive very good treatment and good food. The prisoners of the French are in a small pen surrounded by barbed wire and receive poor rations. As a result, they all want to become prisoners of the U.S. Army.

Our next hop is to El Acounia Field at Tunis, Tunisia. This field was part of the battleground used by Rommel and his forces in their retreat to the Mediterranean Sea and the evacuation of North Africa. The entire countryside is littered with abandoned guns, planes, war machines of various types, and destroyed buildings. Italian prisoners held at El Acounia do K. P., drive trucks, clean the grounds, and take over various other undesirable details. They are allowed the privilege of going into Tunis on pass. The natives here are mostly Arabs, who prove to be a murdering, swindling bunch of thieves. Quite a number of transient flying personnel have been killed in their beds by these thieving Arabs for just a small haul.

We went to Tunis for about an hour and found it to be a dirty city, overrun with refugees.

Our next hop is over the Mediterranean to go to Goya, Italy. This is a B-24 base, and we receive our first dope on combat. [Airmen] had just returned from a mission over the Balkans, and their losses for the day were six planes of a group of twenty-seven sent out. The group was led by a colonel who bailed out in the heat of the fight. The rest of the crew with him flew back to make a safe landing.

Our next hop was to the 99th bomber group, Foggia, Italy. We were met by [someone in] a truck and carried to our squadron where we were drilled for some time with innumerable questions by the flying personnel, who had been away from the states for a long time. After eating, we pitched the tent which was to be home during our stay there.

Life in the squadron was dull. About three afternoons a week we had a softball game, and one night a week we played "bingo." The movie was an outdoor arrangement and only got old reels that we usually had seen before. We played ping-pong in the non-coms club, and the rest of our time was spent reading and writing, or just doing nothing.

Our non-coms club got a few Coca-Colas and beer, but usually had only Italian wines, cognac, brandy, and gin. Our mess hall was clean, but we got only "C" rations which is poor food to fly high altitude missions on.

We had an Italian barber and paid him ten cents for a haircut. We had hot water for showers, and I took one each day.

In our tent we had a stove in which we burned 100 octane gas and cooked eggs bought from Italians. We carpeted our dirt floors with old rugs to keep things cleaner. We slept on canvas cots under mosquito bars.

After a few days in the squadron, we are listed for our first mission. This mission was to targets near Rome. Our job was to destroy supply dumps of the German army in an attempt to disrupt their organization and supply to the front. We didn't drop our bombs through the existing overcast since our troops were nearby and a small error could prove disastrous to our own men. We encountered no flak or fighters, so our mission was not counted toward the required number.

Following this attempt, we made missions to Weiner Neustadt, New Vienna, Austria; Munich, Germany; Budapest, Hungary; Ploesti, Romania; Brod, Yugoslavia; Sofia, Bulgaria; Modena, Italy; Lyons, France; and Regensburg, Germany. Germany's Air Force was depleted at this time, and attacks by German fighters not frequent. They grouped their fighters each day and would hit one or two groups in force. Other groups could not be attacked. The system was to catch the cripples after our planes came off bomb runs and out of flak.

As soon as one of our planes lost an engine, or for some other reason had to leave formation, he would get jumped by fighters.

Flak was the larger problem as a whole. Our only mission free of flak was the last when shot down by fighters. In eleven missions we had received over two hundred flak holes in our plane, varying in size from the size of a quarter to two feet in diameter. Someone saw us through as not one of our crew was injured.

There is no way to describe aerial combat. When your pals go down, you want to feel sorry for them, but have no time for it. There's nothing to compare it with.

After one mission that is rough, an airman has a heart of stone. He might always have an inward fear but develops a hard outward appearance.

He sees death without flinching.

Last Mission July 2, 1944

At 4:30 a.m. our squadron is awakened by the ring of an alert bell coming in a series of short buzzes over the PA system.

We climb out of our canvas cots and into our ground flying suits. We then dash to the mess hall for army "C" rations breakfast of dehydrated eggs, fat bacon, bread, oatmeal, and G. I. coffee. After a second cup of coffee and a cigarette, we load on trucks and go to briefing. After everyone is seated, Lt. Col. Barnett, our twenty-nine-year-old group commander, comes out to give us our target for the day. After receiving an estimate of flak guns and fighters to expect over the target, and our initial point [IP], bombing altitude, target time and other details, we again load on trucks and go to our baggage room to pick up flying equipment.

Dot Day and Barbara Gaddy

We then go to our planes, which we check thoroughly, install machine guns, load ammunition, check oxygen load, regulators and hoses, check interplane stations, turret operation and various other details. Each man has a definite job to do and is responsible for the condition and operation of certain parts of the plane. My responsibility lay in the guns, ammunition, turrets, bombs, bomb racks, stations, and electrical system.

After all is made ready, we put on our heated flying suits and fleece-lined leather flying suits. For the next 30 or 40 minutes we sit on the hard stand under the nose of the plane and talk. Everyone agrees that it should be an easy mission, and we are adding it to our previous total with no feeling of the possible failure to return.

The time comes for starting engines, so we climb aboard and warm up the engines. Our turn to taxi out to the runway follows, and we jockey into position to await take-off. We are the leading squadron of the group and our plane's position is left wing of second element. We are the fifth plane off and climb in a circle around the field until the group is in formation.

During this time (about one hour), everyone makes a final check on all operating equipment, smokes a couple of cigarettes, and wonders how rough the mission will be. Finally, we leave the coast of Italy, climbing as we cross the Adriatic Sea for a high altitude before reaching enemy territory. Just as we get in sight of the Yugoslavian coast, we reach an altitude of 25,000 feet. There is quite a bit of talk over the interphone, such as: "There goes a B-24 home at 9 o'clock low," or "Number three ship first element, second group just feathered number four and is turning back."

The bombardier says, "Enemy land in sight ... armorer, remove pins now, ... all crew call in for an oxygen check and put on your flak suits anytime now."

Laudner, the tail gunner for the day says, "Tail gunner, Rodger." Right waist, left waist, lower ball gunner, radio gunner, upper turret

Battles: Glimpses of Truth

gunner, navigator, pilot, and copilot answer in rapid succession. After this, there is very little said until we get inside of Budapest.

The B-24 groups had already been over Budapest and left many fires and smoke billowing up to approximately 20,000 feet. Our escort over Hungary was P-38s, and we saw quite a number of dogfights with our 38s hauling down quite a number of ME-109s.

First, you would see a 109 and shortly afterwards a P-38 gradually closing the gap between them. When the 38 came into firing range, you [would] see a stream of smoke from the 109 as she started her earthward plunge.

We circled to east of Budapest where we struck our I. P. About this time, we had a good view of burning targets in Budapest which were quite something. Flames belched and leaped three or four hundred feet into the air; [we] encountered some rockets from ground guns, but lost no ships. We circled on north of Budapest, where we struck our I. P. About this time, we had a good view of burning targets in Budapest, which were quite something. Flames belched and leaped three or four hundred feet into the air, sending heavy boiling black smoke already up to 20,000 feet. Our I. P. is a small town eight minutes from target, which is an old refinery on the Danube, fifty miles upstream from Budapest.

We climb into our flak suits and hug to any armor plating we have, as flak starts coming up to greet us. Just after leaving the I. P. our number four engine starts smoking and losing manifold pressure. We open bomb-bay doors as we near the target. The added drag, causing more strain on engines, causes number four to give off a heavier column of smoke. We are ordered to bomb visual and pass over target, while clouds are obscuring. We start a 360° circle in hope of catching a break in the clouds the next time around. The flak is moderate and a bit inaccurate. Number four loses from 46-inch manifold pressure down to 23, which is almost no help.

We start over target again, and number one starts losing pressure due to a burst oil line caused by overload and high operating power setting. The target is still obscured, and we start the second 360° circle. Due to loss of power, we start gradually dropping behind. Edler, our engineer, works fearlessly over [the] Supercharger inverter in an attempt to get some power back. It is of no use, so he tells the pilot get rid of the load. Reuse, our pilot, calls Waller, and he salvos our bomb load. By this time, we are underneath the last squadron of the group and losing altitude as well as dropping farther behind. We pass over the target the third time, and it is still obscured.

Our secondary target is Brod, Yugoslavia, so they head due south for Brod. We are behind the last plane in the group and losing altitude, so they pull off and leave us. Having one engine completely gone and the prop feathered and another pulling only half of what it should, there's only one choice and that is drop down on the deck and hope we aren't attacked.

When we drop to about 19,000 feet and are still going down, all of a sudden 20 copilot bullets started shredding our plane. Two 109's [Messerschmitts] have come up on the tail at 6 o'clock low from within cloud banks and are right on us before we notice.

I, as well as other crewmembers, am inclined to believe our tail gunner was watching our bad engines for a split second; and when he did see the fighters, they were almost on us and peeled away before he could fire his guns. They came in again from the tail, and this time shot the props off number one engine already pulling 23 inches. A 20mm exploded squarely in the top and center of the cowl of number two, so it had to be feathered. Number four was already useless and feathered.

One 20mm burst right on my ammunition belt, knocking me flat on the floor of the plane. The concussion was something terrible. My flak suit saved my life, as it caught the largest pieces of shrapnel. A few small pieces pierced the flying equipment and hit me in the arm, leg, front, and left side. I didn't know that I had received wounds until floating down in the chute. Our P-38s came in and took care of the 109s in the prescribed manner. We dumped everything overboard.

We were losing altitude very fast, and our number four engine had dropped out of the wing after the fire melted the mounting flanges. By this time our altitude had decreased to something like 12,000 feet. The right wing was enveloped in flames and any second [they] reach the gas tanks, which would cause the plane to disintegrate.

Lt. Reuse ordered us to bail out with no other alternative for a decision. We should have gone out earlier. Laudner was first out. His guns had been knocked out, and his face was full of splintered glass; so, he had come up to the waist and was closest to the door. I gave the emergency door release handle a jerk. The door flew off. Laudner, Erickson, myself, Bachman, and Sughrue went out in split-second intervals. Edler, Redding, Waller, Stockton, and Reuse followed from the bomb bay and nose hatch. Reuse amused us by having taken time to pull off his flying helmet and put on an old beat-up garrison hat he had worn practically every day since we left Salt Lake.

Reuse left the ship trimmed at a descending altitude, and it kept going straight away, then turned to the right, starting a circle. This didn't look so good, but she soon settled back and went farther away from us. Erickson, Laudner, and I were close enough to yell at each other on the way down. I told them to first bury their chutes, and then we would get together. Laudner hit about 600 yards north of the small village, after being shot at by a rifle, which missed him.

Erickson landed about 200 yards northeast of the village, and I skimmed a housetop and crashed into a tree, tumbling down through it to hit the ground rather easy. I found myself suspended by my chute, which hung in the branches.

This was about thirty yards from the main street of town, on the backside of an open vacant lot. However, it was not vacant after a few seconds, as all the people in town formed a semi-circle around me. They numbered about 200 strong, and all were armed with some form of farm implement: mostly scythes, hoes, rakes, axes, and so forth. A few carried guns. Someone in the crowd said, "Pistil?" and I shook my head. Some old man mustered up enough courage to come up pretty close and made motions for me to remove my heated suit extension cord.

They were so sure something would explode if they touched anything. Finally, by motioning, patting over my body and removing a few things, they came on up to me and took my watch, escape kit, cigarette lighter, cigarettes and class ring. I had already lighted a cigarette while waiting for them to decide that nothing was going to explode. One guy tried to slip off my wedding band, but I clenched my fist and avoided him for the time being.

They slipped the rope over my head, tied ropes on my wrist, and the three big dogs of town paraded me in front of twenty to thirty civilians who all spit on me down the main street to the building to which they carried me to wait until the others were brought in.

Erickson was brought in right behind me, and Laudner, Waller, Bachman, Reuse, Redding, Edler, Soghrue, and Stockton, in that order. I was laid on a table, and the rest sat along the wall. Again I felt someone trying to take my wedding band. Some German soldiers and a Hungarian, who was authorized by the Germans to supervise that district, came in and one of the German soldiers spoke a little English. I told him to tell the civilian to leave my ring alone, as it was not government property. He made him go away, and I was surprised.

They gave us fat meat and black bread, plus cookies from a lady. The Hungarian commander had to show off in front of civilians by kicking, slapping some of the fellows and making them stand up. He also made them open the escape kits and inflate the Mae Wests to see that they contained no explosives. They knew nothing about flying equipment and after asking a few questions,

Battles: Glimpses of Truth

to which they got no answers, they loaded us into the wagon and took us to another village on the railroad.

We were herded into an old stockade and given a mess kit of potatoes, which didn't appeal to us, due to having lost any appetite we may have had. We were then carried to the train and were spat upon and cursed all the way to the station. We went into a compartment on a third-class passenger car. The windows and doors were locked, and four guards placed there with us. They kept telling us that the war was finished for us and we weren't too sure what they meant. We smoked the last two cigarettes among the ten of us.

We traveled about twenty kilometers to Page, Hungary, where we were taken to a training post in the city. As we walked along, hundreds of civilians mobbed alongside spitting and cursing, but were held off by the guards. My foot was badly swollen and very sore, and I thought we would never get there. Loss of blood from my wounds, in addition to having given a pint of blood to the Red Cross the previous day, had left me pretty weak.

After standing for some time, we were searched and led to our cells, which were dark and musty. Each had a little window at the top of the outer wall, with steel shutters closed over it on the outside.

The door was wood, some four inches thick. The bed was just boards laid over two sawhorses. Being so exhausted, I fell into a deep sleep, but woke up cold. The rest of the night was snatches of sleep, as I lay shivering from cold and eaten by bedbugs.

Reuse and Stockton were put in a cell together, Waller and Redding, Sughrue and Bachman, Edler, Erickson, and Laudner. I had been the only one in a cell by myself. After continued knocking on the door, I finally got it open to go to the latrine. While I was out, Edler, Erickson, and Laudner got out. They changed guards, so I went back in the cell with them, and the guards didn't know I had made a change.

Dot Day and Barbara Gaddy

Our breakfast consisted of ersatz coffee, made of parched rye and acorns, and a slice of black bread. Foul as it tasted, we were hungry enough to eat.

Days passed very slowly as we were very hungry at all times. At noon and at night meals we would get about one teacup of dehydrated greens, soup or beans. With each meal we got a slice of black bread. We bummed a little tobacco and cigarettes from the guards and kids who brought our chow. Quite a few of the boys were Czechoslovakian. We had them believing Laudner was Slavic, and they would bring tobacco and extra chow for that reason.

On July 14, the B-17s came over, and the soldiers dived into their underground shelters. We were looking out the windows and laughing at them, so one old soldier came inside, whipped out his saber as if he were going to kill somebody, but ended up by taking away the sawhorses that we laid planks across for a pretense of a bed.

The next day they told us that our planes had bombed Budapest and quite a number were shot down. They claimed that the fingers were cut off all bombardiers caught there. Some even told us we would be killed when we got to Budapest; another said we wouldn't.

On July 17 we were put on a train boxcar and taken to Budapest. When we got off the train there, we were spat upon and cursed and saved by the guards with us. We were taken then to the civil prison where some one hundred airmen and thousands of Jews were held.

We were put in a bastille with cells about six feet wide and ten feet long. Edler and I were put together. Time passed slowly for us, and we stayed hungry. For breakfast we had a cup of hot water with paprika and a few croutons in it. At noon we had a cup of pea soup, bean soup, dehydrated vegetables or sweetened bread dough. Supper was one of the same. Each day we got a little chunk of bread, about half a pound.

Battles: Glimpses of Truth

We cut us a checkerboard on the bottom of the drawer in a little table and played several games each day. We averaged about sixteen hours sleep a day. They didn't let us out of the room during our entire time. For eighteen days we didn't smoke. When we yelled out windows to fellows in other cells, we were threatened with our lives, but managed to get a little news occasionally.

On August 5 Edler and I were interrogated. We told our names, ranks and serial numbers. An interrogating officer told us about everything else there was to know about our squadron, crew, group, and wing.

On August 7 Edler, Laudner and I left. At the railroad yard we went through the spitting and cursing process again. Finally, we were loaded into a boxcar, twenty-five of us with six Gerry guards. One of the guards was a Polish fellow 65 years old, who had been forced to fight for the German army. We reached Vienna early the next morning and sat in the railyards until 2 p.m. This was a clear day, and we really were sweating out the bombers. From Vienna we went up through Czechoslovakia; Breslau, Germany; Posen, Poland; Frankford on the Oder, Germany; New Stettin, Belgrade, and Gross Tychow, which was three kilometers from camp.

We waited at the station until guards with police dogs came from camp. They started us off marching, speeding us up to a trot, then turned the dogs loose. I really poured on the coal and stayed up at the front of the group, as the ones in the rear were getting bayoneted, bitten, and hit with rifle butts.

I got rammed in the back with a rifle, but stayed out of the reach of the guards after that. Our bunch didn't get nearly as rough treatment as some other groups who came in. One boy got 68 bayonet stabs in the back and legs. Those who had anything with them had to throw it away in an attempt to outrun the guards. No one ever got anything back.

We stayed in Fore Lager the first night and were given plenty of bread, butter, eight cans of Spam and a big pot of English tea. We

Dot Day and Barbara Gaddy

all had such little contracted stomachs that two sandwiches filled us. We slept well. The next morning we moved into the main lager.

Life in the lager was not too bad. We played softball and touch football to pass the daylight hours. We stayed in tents until cold weather, then moved into barracks and slept on the floor. This overcrowded the rooms as they were built for sixteen and we had twenty-four in the room. We had two tables and three stools. Our mattresses were heavy paper stuffed with wood fiber. The men who had bunks were allowed four slats each. This made a very rough and uncomfortable bed. I was glad to sleep on the floor.

Our meals consisted of breakfast: 1 cup of ersatz coffee, at least an excuse for coffee, made from acorns and rye. Lunch: a cup of dehydrated greens, carrots, or turnips. Dinner: one cup of Irish potatoes every day. With this we received one-sixth of a loaf of bread and one twenty-fourth of a pound of oleomargarine every day. We received one half of the weekly Red Cross parcel each week.

Our biggest problem was the fleas and lice. They were uncontrollable due to lack of insecticides. Another problem was scabies, a form of itch resulting from lack of citric acid.

In October we received musical instruments, books, clothing, playing cards, and other needs from the Red Cross. Life became brighter as time passed faster. Two weeks of October we spent in diphtheria quarantine in our room. We started getting letters from home occasionally, and that meant a lot to all.

Also, we had two Protestant padres and a Catholic father for Sunday worship services and two British and two American medical officers.

In January, one of our own boys lost his mind, and for several days afterward everyone seemed tense, thinking that he might be next to lose his.

Our days were rather long during the winter as weather didn't permit staying out of the building for many minutes.

Battles: Glimpses of Truth

The March

February 6th: Left camp at 8 a. m. and marched thirty kilometers with a forty-pound pack and Red Cross parcel. Quite a few men threw away part of their parcel since they expected to go to Belgard and then by train. Many feet were swollen, blistered and raw. We were pushed into a couple of large barns in the dark.

February 7th: Hot water and a breakfast of Red Cross food. Marched twenty-five kilometers. Slept in small barns after the hot water and Red Cross food.

February 8th: Hot water, twenty-five kilometers. Got sick with ptomaine. Hot water on arrival. Very sick. We could still get no information as to our destination.

February 9th: Sick, couldn't eat a thing. Jerries gave hot water and four small potatoes. We stayed in the barn all day.

February 10th: Traded coffee for one-half loaf of bread and a cup of soup. Walked twenty-five kilometers.

February 11th: Walked thirty kilometers. Our ration was one twenty-seventh of a can of corned beef, one-eighth of a pound of butter, one-tenth of a loaf of bread. We piled into barns.

February 12th: We walked thirty kilometers. Spuds that night. We swiped some onions near a barn. Rained on us all day.

February 13th: No water. We ate a box of hardtack, one-ninth of a can of corned beef, one-sixth of a pound of butter, a cup of noodle soup, spuds. Walked forty-five kilometers in rain, sleet, hail, snow, and winds. We walked until 12 midnight in pitch dark, holding the man ahead to stay on the road. A miserable day, many suffered terribly, but managed to keep moving to preserve life. We slept in a rain-soaked open field.

February 14th: we had one-fifth of a Red Cross parcel. Crossed the Oder by ferry at Swinemunder. Made twenty-eight kilometers. Ate spuds at night.

Dot Day and Barbara Gaddy

February 15th: Traded coffee for three quarters of a loaf of bread. We walked twenty-six kilometers. Nothing to eat. We got cold water for the first time in 48 hours.

February 16th: Hot and cold water. I traded coffee for a loaf of bread from the Germans.

February 17th: Moved twelve kilometers and rested the rest of the day. We had spuds to eat.

February 18th: Hot water, spuds, soup. We rested all night. Shaved and washed up. Got sick again with dysentery.

February 19th: Twenty-two kilometers. Spuds and hot water.

February 20th: Laying over. We ate spuds, raw cabbage. No water all day. I'm still sick.

February 21st: Raw cabbage, two-fifths of a loaf of bread, one-fifth of a pound of butter, hot water, kohlrabi soup. We moved eighteen kilometers.

February 22nd: Hot water. Walked twenty-eight kilometers, eighteen kilometers between 3:30 and 7:30 p.m. Nothing on our arrival in Berlin. Many roadblocks in the area.

February 23rd: We marched thirty kilometers. Spuds, water.

February 24th: Marched twenty-three kilometers. Spuds, water.

February 25th: Laid over for rest getting until March 1. No bread and a cup of soup twice a day. Washed up, shaved, and tried to delouse.

March 2nd: Gerry brew. Moved twenty-three kilometers. Spuds at night.

March 3rd: Spuds and water, two-fifths of a loaf of bread and one-tenth of a block of butter for six days. Twenty-one kilometers. Spuds, hot water.

March 4th: Hot water. Thirty-two kilometers. Moved through Waren, Bavaria. It snowed all day. We ate spuds and drank hot water. Boleware sick.

Battles: Glimpses of Truth

March 5th: Spuds. Moved through Malchow near Karow. Had an air raid. We saw the bombers. It was a pretty day, and our spirits were up a bit. We made thirty kilometers.

March 6th: Walked twenty-five kilometers in the mud. Spuds and water. Sixteen hundred left of two thousand who started. Twenty percent of the remainder are sick and riding in wagons.

March 7th: Laying over. Spuds and hot water, kohlrabi soup, two fifths of a loaf of bread. Guys are being returned who tried to escape. Some were killed by SS officers. Men dying from starvation, gangrene, and pneumonia.

March 8th: Marched nineteen kilometers. Spuds and barley soup.

March 9th: Hot water. We are laying over. We ate spuds, 2/5 of a loaf of bread and one-fourth block of butter.

March 10th: Hot water, cup of soup, spuds. Laying over.

March 11th: Hot water, spuds, soup. We had church services by a barn. Air raids day and night.

March 12th: Twenty kilometers. Spuds, barley soup.

March 13th: Twenty-two kilometers. Hot water.

March 14th: Twenty-five kilometers. Hot water.

March 15th: Laying over. Spuds and kohlrabi.

March 16th: Laying over. Water and barley.

March 18th: Services by a barn. Soup.

March 19th: Twenty-seven kilometers. Gerry brew, three-tenths of a loaf of bread and one-tenth of a block of butter.

March 20th: Twenty-five kilometers. Soup, chicken feed, and barley. We crossed the Elbe River.

March 21st: Mint tea. We got a fräulein to boil ten pounds of spuds for soup. They lasted the three of us for three days.

March 22nd: Mint tea, half a can of soup, raw kohlrabi, chicken feed, half a Red Cross parcel. Moved eighteen kilometers. Spuds and hot water. Washed and shaved.

Dot Day and Barbara Gaddy

March 23rd: Laid over. Spuds and water. I washed my socks, underwear, handkerchief, and body. We ate three-tenths of a loaf of bread and one-ninth of a block of butter. Warm and sunny. Russ cut my hair.

March 24th: For food we had grain and ground rye cereal. We made twenty kilometers. Spuds and water.

March 25th: Hot water, soaked rye. Ten kilometers and spuds.

March 26th: Water, sugar beet syrup, one-tenth of a loaf of bread, one-eighth block of butter and hot water.

March 27th: Spuds, horsemeat stew and fresh milk (swiped).

March 28th: Spuds, syrup, and water.

March 29th: Moved by rail from Eybart to Fallings Bostell Camp XIB.

Day 51.

March 30th: Nothing to eat. In a small tent with 200 men. Many lice.

April 1st: Between April 1 and April 8, we had each day a cup of soup (watery), three little spuds each day and one half a Red Cross parcel for the week.

April 9th to 17th: Moving twenty to twenty-five kilometers a day. Cooking our own meals. Rations from the Gerries are a little better.

April 17th: Red Cross and a new lease on life. Up at two a. m. and crossed the Elbe in thirty kilometers hike.

April 18th: Laid over at New Hous. We had beef from the Gerries and plenty of spuds and peas to cook.

April 19th: Moved thirty kilometers to Velan. We were strafed close by. Strafing was meant for Gerry trucks.

April 20th: Laying over. Cooked steak and French fries. We bought fresh eggs.

Battles: Glimpses of Truth

April 21st: We were strafed and bombed. Two killed and twenty-seven wounded. There are many setbacks.

April 22nd: We laid over. Ate well.

April 23rd: Red Cross again. We moved twenty-five kilometers. The bombing is very close.

April 24th: Laid over. Washed my clothes and took bath. Feeling good.

April 25th: Strafing nearby. Lying over. Lots to eat.

April 26th: Strafing nearby. Lying over. Lots to eat.

April 27th: Eating a lot of Red Cross. Sleeping quite a bit. Gerries say it is as good as up.

April 28th: Moved twenty kilometers. Red Cross delivered in White Angels (American Red Cross trucks driven by POWs).

April 29th: Cold. Laying over. One-fourth loaf bread.

April 30th: Cold. Laying over. Typhan (English night bomber thought tanks were in the barn) strafed near barn sending ricocheting bullets through barn, depositing debris on my bed.

May 1st: Moved 3 a.m. Thirty kilometers. Rain, snowed, sleeted, hailed, and rained.

May 2nd: Liberated after 960 kilometers (600 miles).

Liberation at Zarrentin

An English patrol followed by blacks of the Ninth Army. The English kept moving except one officer, who stopped to say that we could start back down the road.

They tossed us candy, oranges, canned meats, cigarettes, bread and crackers. The Jerries threw away their guns. Later, an American officer told us to wait for transportation.

We stayed until the next morning when we took German trucks, cars, wagons, buggies, etc. to leave in.

We four had a car and started out. After passing Boizenburg, we were asked in for a drink and dinner with an American second lieutenant of the MP force. Most all the boys stopped in Boizenburg.

We changed cars – a two cylinder for four-cylinder – and crossed the Elbe to an anti-aircraft outfit where we spent the night after receiving medical attention and a good meal.

The blacks killed 35 Germans in Zarrentin, with up to 50 gun holes in a man. The Kreiges (POWs) looted quite a bit for guns, cameras, field glasses, watches, etc., for souvenirs.

We moved on to Hanover the next day and reported to military government. We were interviewed by a press correspondent and had our pictures taken.

Military government sent us on down to Hildeshem. We carried a couple of aircrew men, spending their pass by visiting the front, down to keep our car on arrival.

We were fed K rations and ten in one (ten men's rations in one box). We slept on the floor in an old vacant barrack. I could barely whisper and still ran a fever.

The next day we had two meals of C rations, were deloused, got new shirts, pants, and jackets and moved to another barrack, where we got beds and were comfortable.

We waited until the eighth, when we got a plane and flew to Paris. We stopped long enough for cake, coffee, and gas, then flew on to La Harve.

We went by truck forty or fifty miles to Camp Lucky Strike, arriving at midnight on May eighth. We had a hot shower, clothes deloused and got new fatigues, underwear, and socks, which made us feel very good. We had a sandwich and soup and went to bed at 2:30 a. m. We have completed processing in a two-day run and are ready to be paid and moved to the shipping area.

May 10th to May 16th: Just laying around eating three good meals a day, punctuated by snacks of cheese sandwiches and eggnog, through the courtesy of the American Red Cross.

Battles: Glimpses of Truth

May 16th: We were transported to Le Harve and boarded the *Thomas A. Berry*, a former luxury liner, the *SS Oriente*, which ran from New York to Miami and has been converted to a hospital ship. She is a beauty with wood fittings. She is a sister ship to the *Morro Castle*, which burned in 1934, causing the loss of hundreds of lives and making history as one of the greatest sea disasters.

May 17th: At about 7:30 a. m. we moved from the docks out into the harbor and formed a convoy. At 8 a. m. we started out across the channel. Meals are lovely, with no limit on amount.

May 18: We pulled into South Hampton Harbor and finished loading the ship with sick and wounded – also English war brides. The wives of our fighting men have quite a few babies, including one English girl and baby (mulatto) who is the wife of a black pursuit pilot.

May 19th: We pull out of the docks, form a convoy, and are on our way at 7 p.m. We carried 2,600 passengers, a crew of 350, 508 feet long, displacing 17,000 tons.

May 20th: Water is pretty rough as waves roll over the bow of the ship, which is cruising at about fifteen knots. About seventy-five percent of the fellows have been throwing their cookies today. The flying personnel and ship's crew are about all that aren't sick.

We had turkey for dinner, and I made about three men's shares, due to the amount of sickness.

May 21st: The water is much rougher, most everyone is sick, including many Merchant Marines. So far, I have held my cookies. Movie, *Gaslight*.

May 22nd: The water is a bit smoother, but it's cloudy and cool, making it uncomfortable on deck. The chow is still very good, and I am doing it plenty of justice.

May 23rd: Water somewhat smoother. So far, I haven't been seasick. Chow still very good. I average eating two to three apples and oranges a day, stewed fruit, and fruit cocktail. Movie, *Higher and Higher*.

May 24th: Water still smooth. Slowed to seven knots as one ship had engine trouble.

May 25th: Days passing slowly as I grow more anxious to reach a long-awaited destination. Eating, reading, sleeping, and daydreaming. Movie, *Tales of Manhattan*.

May 26th: Still smooth and moving pretty fast. Now getting New York broadcasts.

May 29, 1945: We came through the Golden Gate, New York, and then we were taken to a camp north of New York City for interrogation. We were taken by troop train to Camp Shelby, Hattiesburg, Mississippi.

HOME

June 2, 1945: I went to Jackson, Mississippi, and was reunited with my wife Syble, and I met my young son, Larry Payne, born while I was in prison camp. We were soon sent to Miami Beach for rest and relaxation. I was then sent to Regional Hospital (formerly Biltmore Hotel) in Coral Gables, Florida, for a minor surgery.

November 1, 1945 I was honorably discharged as a staff sergeant from the U.S. Army Air Force.

In 1946, I went to Mississippi State College and took ninety-nine hours in two years to graduate in February 1948.

My wife and son and I moved to Crystal Springs, Mississippi, and joined my brother Romuel in business at Wright's Motor and Equipment, an automobile, truck, tractor, and farm implement dealer. In 1983 we closed the business, and I retired.

Syble and I had two more children, Debbie and Marty. We also have five grand-children and six great grandchildren. Syble passed away in September 2003. I moved to the Veterans' Administration Nursing Home in Jackson, Mississippi in January 2004. My three children all live in Copiah County, Mississippi, and I see them often.

Battles: Glimpses of Truth

Key Events in Wright's life include the following:

Military History

Enlisted: 5.21.1942

Induction into Active Duty: 8.4.1942 as Aviation Cadet U.S. Air Force

Organization: 348 Bomb Squad 99 Bomb Gp APO 520

B17 Arm Gunner on the "Flying Fortress"

*Date of capture (12th mission): 7.2.1944 for 10 months (Basic Training Guard House: Pace, Hungary; Civil Prison: Budapest; Stalag Luft IV: Grosstychow, Germany; Stalag XIB: Fallings Bostell, Germany)

Missing in Action Letter Received by father on 8.17.44

Honorable Discharge: 11.1.1945 S/Sgt U.S. Air Force

*Injuries: Shrapnel wounds back of arm and leg, foot, left torso resulting from enemy aircraft firing into plane and shells exploding close by.

Medical Complaints After Return: Easily fatigued, cramps often (especially at night), easily winded, some loss of hearing, some loss of vision, skin abrasions heal very slowly, soreness in joints.

Awards

Air Crew Member Badge

European African Middle Eastern Ribbon

5 Bronze Stars

Purple Heart

Air Medal with 2 clusters

Presidential Citation with one cluster

Good Conduct Medal

American Theater of War Ribbon

Victory Ribbon (WWII)

2 Overseas Bars

Caterpillar Club

COACHING TO WIN

Dot Day

My grandson was the tackling dummy that year.

He had almost two years of playing junior high football in south Alabama. His dad was his coach the first year, and Will did get in the game and played well on offense and defense. He did not start; there were no wins; everyone played some. Bill attempted to develop character in his students in an economically challenged area. The school undercut his discipline efforts, did not back up his decisions, and hired a new coach the boosters liked from area park football.

This new, popular coach coached Will his second year. The school did not play by the rules. He was not an employee of the school and answered only to the boosters. There were no school personnel on the bus when they had an away game. Probably problematic: If there had been an accident, I question whether the school insurance would have debated coverage.

Will did not get to keep his number from the preceding year. A boy who had played park ball for the coach wanted to be number 87. Even though he had transferred to the school and was a year younger, he wore 87. On two occasions, during weekly practices, the coach told Will he would be put in the game and was not. Number 87 missed a day of practice each week and started.

Dot Day and Barbara Gaddy

We live approximately four hours away; Will told his mom that he didn't want us to drive that distance and not see him play. (I am in a power wheelchair, and traveling is difficult.) Last game – Will finally got into the game the last four minutes for four plays as defensive tackle. The other team did not score, and Will did his job. The team lost 28-8.

Their team won one game that year. Unfortunately, cheating paid off. At this level of play, there is no film exchange; yet, the coach had a film of the opponents for the players.

The last game had a fight between the teams; Will did not participate.

Character development is crucial at all ages, but it is hard for someone who knows right from wrong to see wrong winning.

What are the possible lessons Will could have learned?

1. Past performance does not matter. Popularity and familiarity are more important.
2. It is okay for an adult to make promises to a child and not keep them.
3. When cheating will make it possible to win, cheat.
4. The outcome is more important than the manner in which one plays – the end justifies the means.

What did Will show he had learned?

1. Keep his head up and do what is required, even though he feels hopeless.
2. God's promises are the important ones. He keeps His.
3. Standing on the sidelines within arm's reach of the coach indicates readiness even if he doesn't get into the game.
4. Standing and waiting is tough; he continued to think of others' difficulties and spared his grandparents.

5. A win means more when it is earned.
6. Because he will continue in athletics this year, he must not complain because the ones in charge might exact a penalty.

I don't know what Will learned about forgiveness. In my seventh decade, I often want to confront problems by bringing them to others' awareness. Maybe I am putting myself in the role of the Holy Spirit. Maybe there is a vindictive me who wants to pass a note to the coach, "Karma knows what you did. You will pay." To me, karma does not exist, but I think the coach would fear "What goes around, comes around" more than the stirrings of the Holy Spirit to a more character-building approach.

Now, my belief is in a loving heavenly Father. I count on His mercy and grace. Yet, I despise those who mislead children and young people. The smart thing for me is not to offer sympathy but to remind Will of the advantages he has had in a loving and supportive home, having a Christian walk and background.

Will is a wonderful young man, smart, handsome, humorous. His time will come. He does not have to be the best player on the team, but I do want him to be the best Christian witness in a public-school culture where there are few practicing Christian disciples. So far, by God's grace, he shows great character.

MEDICAL MISSIONS
Philip Levin, M.D.

America offers opportunities and luxuries unimaginable in underdeveloped countries. Plentiful food and water, marvelous shelters, and a safety health care network provide our citizens with an underappreciated fulfillment of our basic needs, and so much more. Citizens in many other nations are not as fortunate.

The last of my three children left for college in 2004, relieving me of the responsibility of being a single parent. With the skills and training of twenty-six years of emergency medicine, I recognized the opportunity to fulfill a dream I'd always had of being a medical missionary. I knew of one of my fellow ER physicians, Dr. Killebrew, who went with the Episcopalians to a village in the Honduran mountains each year. He had decided to skip that year, so I arranged to take his place.

The mission in Honduras had been ongoing for a dozen years, spending a week there each May. Earlier groups had built a few facilities: dormitories for the volunteers, showers, a dental clinic, and a pharmacy. Our group included three physicians, three dentists, a veterinarian, and eight other helper volunteers. We arrived in San Pedro Sula where we were met by the advance team and loaded up the crew and supplies into two buses and a truck. From there we left the paved roads of the city to wind up narrow mountain

Dot Day and Barbara Gaddy

dirt roads, over flooded creeks and arrived at a small village whose name I've forgotten. We were welcomed there by big banners stretched across the one road, and a crowd of three dozen villagers.

Living conditions there introduced me to the rigor of future missions. The sleeping arrangements offered primitive thin mattresses on squeaky, bumpy springs in a dorm with a dozen other volunteers. Cold water showers came in dirty bath facilities. Food could be adequate, though often sparse. Roosters crowed all night; sleeping with white noise blasting through my headphones gave the only chance for dreams.

Dentists provided the most health care. They had an efficient system of pulling teeth, with a friendly competition as to who would pull the most in a day. The vet commandeered a horse – I don't know where he got it – and made rounds by horseback to farms near and far, vaccinating animals and providing other necessary care.

We three physicians set up in the village community center, a translator for each of us. The area villagers lined up by the hundreds to see us, many walking barefoot for dozens of miles in the pre-dawn hours. Old men hobbling on canes, mothers with five children in hand and another in a papoose, and young workers in t-shirts and slacks, gathered in groups in the town square to await our services. Unable to do any tests, we provided evaluations and advice, with our stock of medications running out within three days. Our most useful treatment was a measured dose of a drug called Ivermectin which targeted parasites, specifically bedbugs, an inherent and apparently universal issue. A single dose prevented the creatures from biting for six months! In America, the drug was only approved for use in horses.

Every evening after we'd finished seeing patients for the day, we'd gather in the church for a service thanking God, a few of the villagers joining in the hymns with loud melodic voices. On our

Battles: Glimpses of Truth

last evening, Saturday night, we had a pig roast and a dance, with local mariachi musicians providing a raucous revelry.

Why did this mission affect me so strongly? Certainly, it wasn't because I was saving lives. I could have done more of that in my home ER. However, while there would always be a doctor in my home hospital, my presence on the mission provided care for hundreds who otherwise would have had none. This adventure taught me the joy of giving of myself without expecting any rewards beyond a thank-you.

That was the first of my ten missions. For the second, in 2006, I journeyed into the Amazon River basin to volunteer at a malaria clinic on a river only accessible by boat. I learned how to read malaria on slides and the basics of treatment. Repeat customers were common, although malaria wasn't as prevalent there as in many other parts of the world. Partly this was because of the lower population density. There are four types of malaria in the world. South America doesn't have the most vicious type, Falciparum.

The malaria clinic was set up by a family physician from Wisconsin. By the time of my visit, she'd run it by herself for several years, accepting the occasional volunteer such as me. Since then, she's accepted local physicians to help out and also obtained a Peruvian medical license. Malaria is responsible for about a half million deaths worldwide yearly, and even if it doesn't kill, its rigors, fever and chills, sweating, and body aches can make the victim wish it had.

In 2008 I searched the Internet looking for a mission opportunity and discovered that the Mercy Ships organization was seeking volunteers for an onshore medical mission in suburban Maputo, the capital of Mozambique. Mozambique had once been a prosperous economic and agricultural breadbasket, a well-run Portuguese colony. That ended with the revolution for independence which lasted for fifteen years, from 1977-1992. In 2008 it ranked as one of the ten poorest countries in the world, with the seventh highest

Dot Day and Barbara Gaddy

infant mortality. One out of ten children born alive would die before age one.

This was my first exposure to deep poverty. In the area where we set up, we found families, mostly a woman with her children, living on a small parcel of land, about twelve by twenty feet. The lots had small concrete shacks, usually without windows. Some had a small vegetable garden, and a few had an occasional rooster running about. For water the villagers tapped the underground pipes.

We set up in an orphanage, a two-acre piece of scrub that held four crumbly buildings, a soccer field, and an old green truck. Our group consisted of two physicians, three nurses, a physical education specialist, an assistant pharmacist, a spiritual leader, and some teenagers. The thirteen women stayed in a dormitory and I, the only male, holed up in an outdoor storage shed just large enough to hold my bedroll.

The morning after our arrival, six of us took a neighborhood stroll, walking a few blocks and introducing ourselves through the translators. We told them about our mission and that it would open the gates in two hours. Word of mouth spread the news, and we found at our portal over two hundred families.

I remember one child, a four-year old. He'd been hit by a car several months before, with a resultant compound lower leg fracture, bones sticking out through the skin. Although the local witchdoctor had tried his best, the child had developed osteomyelitis, a bone infection. The child's mother had carried him a mile from a neighboring village and waited for two hours in the African sun to have me examine him. What he needed was IV antibiotics and perhaps surgical intervention. What he would get instead was an eventual amputation. It broke my heart to tell her I couldn't help her child.

Here I learned how I could live without luxuries. I slept in a stifling shack with insects crawling and flying about. We ate what

Battles: Glimpses of Truth

the orphans had to give, a cup of rice with some greens mixed in. I lost several pounds until I discovered a neighborhood store selling Fanta orange, with which I obtained enough sugar to maintain my caloric needs.

Most importantly, I understood I could practice medicine with the minimum of supplies, relying on my experience and empathy.

I had bonded with the other physician on the trip, a Malaysian-born Australian family physician I'll call Tamal. I thought I was tough, but the stories she told of her mission adventures, like the one where the revolutionaries kidnapped her on East Timor, well … I didn't even want to try to top them.

The following year Tamal emailed me to see if I wanted to join her for a mission in Turkey. I had to beg off because it came on the same week as my son's graduation from college, and, well, one does have to have priorities. The following year, though, she found a place in Kenya for us, and 2010 saw the start of my most intensive project.

Kisii, Kenya, is a small town, the capital of the county also called Kisii, which has a population of over a million. At the time, the town consisted of a row of a dozen concrete buildings used as shops along the main road running from Nakuru in the east to the Lake Victoria resort of Kesumu. There's one side street with a butcher shop, car repair spot, and a small restaurant, and one block north of the road, up the hill, sits the county hospital.

The people there were always grateful, always happy, and desperately poor. The average daily wage in Kisii when I was there was forty cents. Most homes had no electricity or running water. Vendors sat at a table on the main street all day selling bananas at ten cents each, hoping to sell four during the day.

Kenya ranks the services available at their hospitals from one, the barest of clinics, to five, a full-scale hospital only available in Nairobi. Kisii's hospital ranked a three, with eight wards, family planning and immunization clinics, and obstetrical services. The

Dot Day and Barbara Gaddy

medical services constructed an x-ray building in 2010, but never completed it or supplied it with equipment. A surgical suite was built in 2011, but Kisii hadn't a surgeon or an anesthesiologist or the supplies to run it.

The hospital served roughly 100,000 people, seeing about 100 walk-in patients a day, and hospitalized up to 40 at any one time. We had a choice of twelve lab tests, although we rarely ran any besides malaria and typhus, for the patients couldn't afford to pay for tests. We didn't touch any of our patients, for the hospital had no running water to wash our hands. We had a choice of three antibiotics and a handful of other medications.

In the pharmacy they had scores of little bottles of liquid amoxicillin and Tylenol sitting next to each other, separated by a piece of cardboard. Each bottle was a different shape, dependent on the patients bringing back old shampoo bottles or such to fill. Both of these drugs are pink liquids, and I wondered how often the wrong one was dispensed.

The medical records department had no file cabinets. Stacks of medical records filled shelves and created towers on the floor. All of the last names started with K, M, N, or O; no one had a government number, and birthdates were usually uncertain. Although I wondered how they found the needed chart, the clerks always located the right one.

About two thirds of our patients had malaria. Most of those could be treated with outpatient medicine, a three-day course of pills taken twice a day. However, very young children and those in whom the disease had great intensity required admission and IV therapy for a day or two. Malaria is transmitted by the bite of an infected mosquito, endemic to the area. As our hospital was open air, that is, all the windows were open, mosquitos came and bit the patients while they were admitted, reinfecting them.

The hospital was staffed by clinicians, U.S. equivalents of licensed vocational nurses (LVNs), who had a year of training and

Battles: Glimpses of Truth

then a year of internship. There were two steady staff and a midwife plus a new intern each of my trips. In its twenty-year history, the arrival of my friend and me marked the first time they'd had physicians. We made rounds each morning and staffed the clinic in the afternoons. Making diagnoses without lab tests meant using experienced judgments; but even so, treatments were limited. I remember one case where the clinician had admitted a patient she had diagnosed as having cellulitis due to the patient's leg being swollen and red. On my exam I diagnosed, instead, a blood clot in the patient's leg. The hospital had no blood thinners, no coumadin, and certainly nothing as sophisticated as heparin, so all we had to treat the patient with was an aspirin a day.

I learned a lot about tropical medicine, seeing firsthand diseases I'd never seen in America: typhus, brucellosis, typhoid fever, cholera, and, of course, lots of malaria.

From the moment I left my home on the Mississippi coast, the trip to the Kisii hospital took sixty hours. Three plane trips took me to Nairobi with overnight stays in Europe, followed by an eight-hour bus ride to the town. I stayed in an orphanage about four kilometers from the hospital, down muddy roads impassable to automobiles after a rain. Sometimes I'd hike the hour to or from, or more often I'd hire a motorcycle taxi called a boda boda for $2.

The orphanage was run by a pastor whose wife was a schoolteacher. He had too much of an open heart. The first year I stayed in his place he had nine orphans, the second year, fourteen. By the fourth year there were thirty-nine. On the second year I paid for electrical wiring and plumbing for the orphanage, and so by the third trip could enjoy a hot shower. Big improvement.

After my first year, I determined that I would return and install running water for the hospital. I had taken plenty of photos on my first trip, including about 800 on a safari. I created a book from these photos, a children's story about a baby elephant, and sold $5,000 worth during the ensuing year. With this money, and more from

55

my pocket, I installed a water supply for the hospital, outfitting new gutters, cleaning the cistern, putting up a water tower, securing a pump, and replacing all the fixtures and toilets. Afterwards we had a great celebration with white bread and Fanta sodas, and they planted a tree in the hospital yard in my honor.

In all I made four trips to this little hospital, 2010, '11, '12, and '14. During each trip I brought gifts, bottles of medicine, CPR dummies for training, my old microscope for their lab, and other leftover supplies from my hospital. In the long run, my legacy might not be much, besides the tree. The water supply breaks down frequently. The drugs ran out. I did put a man through medical school, and he named his child after me. I paid for him to set up his clinic, but with mismanagement it went bankrupt. Still, I helped a lot of people, experienced a bit of the world that few see, and certainly had a marvelous time.

India 2013

In the 1970s there was a leper colony in Louisiana. In 1976, at a medical school in Houston, I saw one of those patients, the only case of leprosy I'd see in my career for the next 37 years. Thus, I jumped at the chance to visit a leper colony in India in 2013.

Leprosy is an infectious disease caused by a very slow-growing bug. It causes nerve damage that results in self-injury, notably loss of finger digits and blindness. Interestingly, it's believed that leprosy can only be caught by children, and only about 10% of people are susceptible. These days it can be cured with thirty days of medical treatment.

I traveled with the Children of the World organization to India: well, I traveled to India with my girlfriend for a ten-day tour of the three Golden Cities, and then met up with the organization. They had an orphanage where they'd paid for a swing set we were inaugurating, and I did some medical examinations and advice with the orphanage.

Then the payoff, a clinic visit to a leper colony.

In the early twentieth century, the government of India set up a colony for the lepers near the large city of Chennai. Some 80 patients who had suffered from leprosy before being cured lived in the compound, each with a small concrete room, about the size of a walk-in closet, with a mattress, a bowl for water, a bowl for food, and two outfits. The six-acre plot also had a temple, a church, and a community hall. A large room contained a workshop with tools designed to be operated by those with no fingers, and a four-stove kitchen offered specially designed cooking gear. Shade trees stood over stone benches throughout the compound, and along a creek monkeys played in large-leaf trees.

The lepers lived a stoic life, subsisting on handouts from the government, unable to work because of their disabilities, usually no fingers and blindness. Yet, most of them were quite happy. I suppose they recognized that given their physical state, the relatively worry-free life they lived was a blessing.

The Children of the World organization had recruited three other Indian physicians and set up tables in the compound for the four of us. We interviewed and examined the patients, offering advice and dispensing medications we'd brought along. I saw for myself another aspect of medicine, one that few other western doctors have witnessed, and which very few others will ever have the chance to see. This disease will be wiped off the face of the planet, another advancement during my time as a physician.

Haiti 2016

At the state medical society meeting in 2015, I enjoyed a conversation with a young physician about mission work. She told me she was in charge of a small group from Tulane Medical School that went to Haiti once a year and operated a walk-in clinic there for a week. I volunteered to be one of the members for the 2016 exhibition coming in the spring.

Our group consisted of seven volunteers, led by a second-year surgical resident. We also had three first-year medical students, a pharmacy student, and my French girlfriend, Isabelle, as assistant and French translator, her first mission trip ever.

I no longer remember the name of the little village, though can describe it: small; very high in the mountains; very, very rural; and very, very, very poor. The populace lived in mud homes that had banana leaves for roofs. The one town pump gathered morning townswomen, each carrying huge jugs to fill for their family's daily needs. The only electricity in the village came from three solar panels originally targeted for the church, but now requisitioned and scattered around town. In the evenings, we seven would sit on the roof of the old church and watch these three points of glow.

We stayed in that old church, a crumbling clay structure of early twentieth-century fame. A board acted as a front door, and our second-floor rooms had no furniture besides ancient mattresses on the floor. In place of window frames, square holes in the walls were covered with slim curtains. In the evening, a generator provided electricity for an hour. The mountain water showers were so cold that one almost preferred to stay dirty. Isabelle and I had a private shower, and the rest shared the other shower. One night we heard two of the female students scream as they discovered a huge tarantula in their shower stall.

Two local villagers had left the town, sought education and success in America, and then decided to return home to help their families and friends. One was a successful businessman responsible for the town's pump and for arranging the medical missions. The other was a veterinarian. He had studied agriculture and was helping the population transition from an economy based on mangos to new crops and projects.

Battles: Glimpses of Truth

I'm going to have to state this up front. If I hadn't been there, the mission would have been a disaster. The head physician, with less than two years of medical experience, was way over his head with the intensity and volume of patients. The three first-year medical students had only had lectures. I'm sure they hadn't expected that they'd be acting like doctors their very first morning in Haiti. With my 38 years of medical experience and several prior mission trips, I was there to instruct and support them, as well as see the bulk of the patients.

In one room we'd set up the pharmacy, a huge collection of somewhat outdated medicines, sorted by types (antibiotics, antihistamines, antihypertensives, etc.). Isabelle and the student pharmacist spent every day in this stuffy, nearly windowless room separating the different drugs and putting pills into little plastic bags to be distributed per our prescriptions.

She remembers, "I was sweating like a pig."

For the first three days, a dozen or so of the townsfolk would wait for us just outside the church gate with handicrafts they hoped we'd buy. When we took breaks, usually for lunch, Isabelle and I would wander out and buy some of their lovely work. We still have a lot of those art pieces, tablecloths, and carvings.

On Saturday evening we attended a prayer session, stuffed into a small building with two dozen others, including French creole songs with dancing and sermons. Afterwards we made our way back to the church illuminated by dim starlight. At one point on our return, our guide turned his flashlight onto the path in front of us and we startled at seeing dozens of tarantulas scurrying away from the light. We had seen these hundreds of holes in the road before, and now we realized each one was the home of one of these huge arachnids.

Meals on mission trips can be interesting parts of the experience. In the church's main hall rested a single table where the food was offered. There were no seats or silverware. Our meals consisted of rice, beans, and mangos. Always mangos. Plenty of mangos. One night we also had fish.

We had arrived via a five-hour miserably hot and bumpy jeep trip. Because of some personal matter that came up at home, Isabelle and I had to leave early. We chartered a small plane to take us to Port au Prince. Enroute we saw how the land had been devastated by prior poor administrations – dusty scrab rock where once had been lush forests.

When we finally settled back into our home, Isabelle took a hot shower that lasted over an hour. She said, "Thank you very much for that experience, Philip. I don't ever want to do it again."

Peru 2017

My tenth medical mission brought me to the outskirts of Cusco, Peru, a city of half a million population in the Andes Mountains. Once the capital of the Inca empire, and later a Spanish colonial regional capital, the lovely town had museums, archeological sites, and history galore. Little stone alleyways wound around the hill-sides, skirting old stone walls and passing among the crowded cobblestone streets. Delightful shops peeked out from every nook, handicrafts and loomed clothing their specialties. Wild gray-furred dogs lounged around the plaza, rib bones showing under loose skin, cowering at a human's approach.

At 11,000 feet elevation, altitude sickness struck immediately to us coastal residents. On my arrival I had to take frequent rests for the first two days, suffering from shortness of breath when climbing the hills. The natives chewed on coca leaves that help a lot, and, in fact, they provided those in big barrels to arriving visitors in the airport. Drinking plenty of water helped, too.

The company that staged the mission arranged residence at the home of a judge. Her hostel had about eight bedrooms, ours being particularly cold and noisy at night, the bathroom supplied with

Battles: Glimpses of Truth

only cold water. After a couple of days of this, we decided to move to a hotel.

For this mission I had arranged to work in a doctor's office high in the hills on the outskirts of the city. My medical Spanish is adequate, so I could follow what he was doing with his patients, and it wasn't much. A government employee, he felt little obligation to help the unfortunate patients assigned to his service, giving them each the briefest of interviews before assigning them a semi-random diagnosis and prescribing them one from a handful of prescriptions he considered his repertoire. After a single day of this, I sought out a different physician, and fortunately found one in the same building willing to have me observe his practice.

This fellow, a man in his 50s, specialized in obstetrics, performing ultrasounds on all his pregnant patients and giving excellent prenatal care and advice. We ran urinalysis and blood counts on all of them, with in-office equipment at minimal costs. About half of his patients were non-obstetrical, and he gave each his best efforts. He kept handwritten records in an unlocked file cabinet. Often the patients' issues were too complex, and he told them honestly he couldn't diagnose them without testing, and he didn't have the ability to run other tests. They would nod, smile, thank him, and return in a few days to see if he had changed his mind.

Once again, I found that a dedicated physician can help many patients, even without supplies or laboratory tests, if he takes the time to listen, examine, and consider the options. We couldn't help everyone, but then again, even in America with all of our sophisticated equipment and incredible intervention possibilities, we can't help everyone either. This Peruvian doctor spent almost no government money, charged the patients nothing, and helped everyone he saw, even if it was only to give them medical advice.

I'll finish this essay with the quote from the back cover of my book, *On a Mission*, a 100-page memoir based on my Kenya trips *(available at www.doctors-dreams.com).*

Dot Day and Barbara Gaddy

"Why would someone choose to be a missionary? What motivates a man with a job and active social life to spend his time volunteering on the other side of the planet? What inspires a woman to leave her comfortable home and, instead, sleep in cramped hot quarters, using filthy bathroom facilities, and eating subsistence food? Ask a missionary why he gives up so much to spend his time and money to help others. Likely, he'll get a dreamy look in his eyes as he remembers the faces of the grateful people he helped. He'll smile, shrug, and say, "I gained more than I gave."

SWIMMING KATRINA
(or Black Lace and Broken Sandals)
Barbara Grillot Gaddy

Editor's note: In 2005 Hurricane Katrina devastated the Mississippi Gulf Coast. Barbara Gaddy, at the time Barbara Harris, worked at Northrop Grumman and wrote the following article for the company newsletter. She served as the manager, IIS Business Planning and Communication. She shared her personal account of escaping her flooding home and swimming to safety during Hurricane Katrina. She survived the ordeal with her husband, Jim, a chemist at Ship Systems, and her son, Daniel, who worked for PFG Precision Optics, Inc in Ocean Springs, Mississippi. (Written by the editor of the company newsletter)

Our house is located in the Fontainebleau area of Ocean Springs, which is located about fifteen miles to the west of Pascagoula. The house is approximately one mile inland from the shore of the Gulf of Mexico. In previous storms, barrier islands and thickly wooded areas surrounding our house took the brunt of the wind and rain, buffering our home from most of the damage. Our house is elevated some five feet above sea level and sits on top of nine-foot pilings, which put the floor of our house approximately ten feet above sea level. During the storm, the water actually rose

Dot Day and Barbara Gaddy

to between six and seven feet *inside* the house, which calculates to one heck of a water rise and surge, about fifteen-twenty feet above sea level. That's why we were swimming out of our house in the middle of a hurricane. (NOAA later documented the water level at our house location to be 22 feet.)

As the storm approached, we were watching the reports of the storm's path, the projected landfall, the anticipated tides and surges and the wind velocity anticipated for our area. We fully expected that we would get very strong winds and rising water like we did during Hurricane Georges in 1998. We had eight feet of water under the house during Georges, but we were okay for all reasonable measures. Bottom line, we weren't naïve about the strength of Hurricane Katrina. We just didn't expect Katrina to be the "mother of all hurricanes!" And neither did the weather forecasters.

Having been through past storms, we have our "preparation planning" down to a fairly streamlined process – pier furniture, patio furniture and tools are brought up to the house level via an elevator we installed when my elderly parents lived with us several years back. Everything is secured and raised to the height of the inside of the house. We move the gas grill onto the front porch so we are able to cook when we lose power, which always happens. We have all the necessary provisions – water, canned food, flashlights, oil lamps and plenty of oil.

What follows are the Blackberry messages that I was sending my daughter and brother on August 29. (I didn't look at them after initially receiving and sending the messages until about a month after the storm.) They are as follows:

5:07 a.m. – Just lost power. Wind is stronger now as you would expect.
5:45 a.m. – (from Angela, my daughter) I hope your battery is charged. Water still rising?
6:02 a.m. – Yes, and really strong winds!

Battles: Glimpses of Truth

6:15 a.m. – Just heard trees falling and cracking.

7:15 a.m. – We just lost the pier and well house.

7:49 a.m. – Water is almost level with the porch now – lots of wave action, very strong winds, lots of trees down – it is really bad! (Note: this means that at this time the water was approximately 10 feet deep, which would be at the porch level.)

9:25 a.m. – (Angela was watching the news in her home in Columbus, Ohio, and sent this message) The levee broke at the French Quarter.

At about 9:30 a. m., the windows in my house started blowing out, and the water was lapping up through the boards on the front porch. I walked into the master bath and the tile was literally floating up from the floor. When we walked back through the bedroom, the water was "squishing" in the carpet. We put our cats (and some food for them!) in the middle of our high king-sized bed, thinking that SURELY the water would not get higher than that bed. Wrong assumption on that one!

By the time we walked back into the den, the water was rising so quickly that the furniture (side tables, chairs, etc.) was beginning to float up and tilt over, spilling items on top. Quickly, the water got knee-deep in the house, and the heavy pieces of furniture (china cabinet, refrigerator, etc.) started falling over. At that point, my husband, Jim, said, "We've got to get out of here!" I frantically began retrieving my photo albums from a bottom shelf in the den and placing them on the couch. Surely the water would not continue to rise to that level! Another wrong assumption!

I remember standing in the middle of the den, turning 360 degrees, just "observing" what was happening around me. I felt as though I were in an IMAX theater, with the action in slow motion. I saw the furniture falling over, the chairs floating, the logs and other debris floating by the large, beautiful plate-glass windows (remember that means the water is approaching 12-13 feet deep at

Dot Day and Barbara Gaddy

this point), seeing the refrigerator float up and fall over, along with a five-foot diamond-shaped island in the kitchen being toppled over into the wall ovens. How was this possible? Then I looked down the long hallway and saw, through the window in the boys' bedroom, a huge wave rolling directly toward the house. Someone, I don't know if it was me or one of the guys, said, "That window is about to blow." And blow it did, the water rushing into the house and down the hallway into the den and strongly surrounding us.

I went to the front door (which was still on the hinges); and when I opened it, the hurricane winds were so tremendously strong that I closed it and told Jim and my son, Daniel, that I wasn't sure if we should try to swim in winds that strong. I wasn't hesitant about the swimming part – just the fierceness of the winds. Daniel replied with quite a chilling statement, "Mom, if you stay in the house, you will be killed in here."

I still had a Blackberry signal at that point, so I made a quick call to my brother to let him know our condition and that we were going to have to swim out. Of course, he was afraid for us to take that chance and was extremely concerned about the risk we were taking. VERY briefly, I explained that we simply had no choice.

The phone call went like this when he answered:

"Hi there, how's it going?"

"Larry, I don't have time to talk. I just want you to know that we are getting ready to swim out."

"Barbara, you can't do that."

"We don't have a choice."

"Do you realize the risk you are taking?"

"Yes. But we really don't have a choice. I need to go now. Just please don't tell Mama what's going on."

My brother and his wife and my elderly mother had traveled from his house in Diamondhead – located to the west of Ocean Springs and 'closer to predicted landfall' per the weathermen – to Crystal Springs, Mississippi, to my Aunt Carol's house to get out of the storm's predicted landfall. I was told later that he paced in my aunt's back yard so much after our call that Aunt Carol (I'm named for her – Barbara Carol) finally went outside and said, "Ok, tell me what's going on. You've been out here all day, pacing." After he finally relayed to her our plight, she joined in prayers for our safety – and I'm certain God heard those prayers. I was not able to get a call through to him until around 8 p.m. that night to let him know that we were safe. When I was finally able to get a call through, Aunt Carol answered, "Hello?"

"Aunt Carol, this is Barbara."

"Oh, thank goodness!" The relief was so audible in her voice. "Here's Larry."

But before that call a lot happened – so back to the part about swimming out!

Immediately after my initial call to Larry, I grabbed my wallet, Blackberry, a few pieces of my special jewelry, and three small books (3" x 4") containing progressive pictures of my three children from birth through high school graduation that would fit in Ziploc bags, and put them in an ice chest that had a handle I could grip easily so that I could tow it out with me. We stepped out onto the porch and into the winds. As I stepped outside, I looked down at my hands and realized I did not have my wedding rings or Cameo ring that my parents gave me for my eighteenth birthday. I told the guys that I had to go back in the house to get my rings from the bathroom counter where I had left them. Of course, they thought I'd REALLY lost my mind.

When I was in the house I also decided that I MUST be properly dressed – for efficient swimming, of course – but also in case my body was later found if the worst scenario played out. I put on my Victoria's Secret black lace bra and matching black lace panties, cut-off jeans shorts, a black tank top, and Teva sandals that are made for tough hikes and water activities.

Dot Day and Barbara Gaddy

As we swam off the porch into fifteen feet of water, the water continued to rise. I saw my Daddy's army trunk floating away toward the open bayou waters. My heart just couldn't take it – and I unthinkingly said to Daniel, my son, "Go get RayRay's trunk." Once again, he thought I'd really "lost it" and asked, "Mom, do you know what you are asking me to do?" I cried as I watched my Daddy's beloved trunk float away. We were swimming INTO the hurricane winds and AGAINST the current, and we could see the white-capped waves breaking through the trees. The pine cones being blown off the forest of pine trees felt like bombs hitting us as we swam. I felt something underneath my feet as I swam and briefly wondered 'what creature am I feeling?' It was only the tree limbs that I was feeling since at that point, in approximately 17 feet of water, I was swimming OVER some of the trees. Sobering realization.

Later, people would ask me if I had been afraid of the alligators that populated the bayou on which our house fronted. My standard answer to them? "All God's creatures were trying to live that day. None of us were worried about the others." And, indeed, as I was swimming, I saw a very large nutria rat taking refuge on a floating piece of wooden debris, trying to rest a bit in the storm.

The wind was so fierce that it continually blew open the lid of the ice chest I was towing as I swam. I'd pause, turn the ice chest around to face the opposite direction, and continue swimming (side-stroke, rescue style as if towing someone) – only to have the swirling wind blow it open again. I prayed, "God, please don't let me lose these last few items that I'm trying to save." And I'd continue my swim, towing my precious memories with me. What was so precious in that ice chest? My co-workers thought I was a "dedicated" employee because I had my Blackberry in double Ziploc bags. Nope – that Blackberry was my only connection to what was the "outside world" – and I knew I'd need it. My laptop? Nope – same reason. The precious objects were three mini photo

Battles: Glimpses of Truth

albums, each measuring three inches by four inches, containing pictures of my three children – Patrick, Daniel, and Angela – from birth pictures through high school graduation photos. I was losing everything else. I just could NOT lose those! Yes, they were also in double Ziploc bags. (I should do commercials for Ziploc and Victoria's Secret!)

We swam approximately a quarter mile – which took us 5-6 hours – toward "high ground" where we had taken our cars, truck, and boat to keep them safe in the storm. Being experienced with hurricane preparations, I had put all my important files, documents, and papers, in heavy plastic file containers – and placed those in the trunk of my car. I'd also put some irreplaceable family photos from ancestors in the car for safe-keeping. After all, the high-ground location had always protected the vehicles from flooding or water damage. I kept wondering, "Where are the cars? It can't be much farther to get to them." Of course, in this case, they were under water at least six feet, along with my insurance papers, birth certificates, other special papers, and those special family pictures I had stashed in the cars.

I finally saw the boat, still trailered to the truck – but with the bow down in the water and the stern floating upward with the rising water. I finally made it to the boat and thought, "I'll get in the boat and out of this nasty water and ferocious wind." To let you know how deep the water was at that location, I am 5'8" tall and I could stand on tiptoe and tilt my head up so my nose was out of the water. But as I tried to climb in the boat, I realized that I was simply too weak at that point to help myself get in the boat – a "simple" task that I'd done so many times with ease. And then I heard someone crying out, "Help! Help us!" I remember thinking at the time how funny that was. I had been swimming for my life for hours, was exhausted, towing an ice chest with just a few precious things, too weak to even get in the boat for safety – and someone wanted ME to help THEM?

The cry for help was coming from a house where several young people were trapped. Remember, the water was still 5-6 feet deep at this point. They had opened the kitchen window to cry out for help when they saw me – and more water poured into their house than had already found its way inside. I vaguely remember calling back to them asking how I could help them. Their answer? "You have a boat. We can get out of here." We were ALL already in shock at that point, because there was no way we could get that boat off the trailer and into any useable position. Desperation ceases all logical thinking at times. And we were desperate.

We made our way to their garage where the doors had been blown off by the hurricane winds. The water was neck deep on me, but it provided us a refuge from the horrific hurricane winds. We stayed there in the contaminated water inside that garage for approximately five hours until the winds died down enough for us to wade back to our house to check the storm damage and destruction. The water was still chest deep at the house when we made it back there. We had to wend our way through the tree limbs and debris to make it there. It was absolutely devastating to see the destruction, and actually, it's fairly amazing that we are alive.

After we investigated the damage and loss, we made our way back to the main road out of the area. There was STILL water to wade through, even on the "high road" locations. I will always remember that there were already "rubber-neckers" out driving through the area – touring around just to see the damage. Now, I know that after the day I'd had, I did not look like I was simply out for a stroll. Those Teva sandals could not withstand the strength of the water and the straps had broken away from the soles during the long swim; so I had on no shoes. I was obviously weary, in shock, and extremely bedraggled. But not a single person stopped to ask if we needed help – a band of three people in this condition! The only person who finally stopped was the Fire Chief. He was in the Fire and Rescue Truck and told us, "I know y'all need help, but I'll have to come back for you later. Right now, I need to get dead bodies out of these houses." Now *that* will help you get your priorities straight. We kept on walking.

I cannot say enough about the friendship, assistance, offers of help, provisions, etc. that Northrop Grumman and its employees and their friends provided. The concern was evident in the efforts made to locate all of our employees. The messages and calls that I received personally are as much the essence of "one Northrop Grumman" as our integration of systems and product support across the company's business sectors.

It will take a very long time even to resemble any sort of normalcy. For the first few weeks, we bounced around from one house to another. We found all four of our cats after a few days. They were very traumatized and were "hospitalized" for a while. We have them back now, and they seem to be doing well. Probably better than we are! Steve Cook, a co-worker from Dallas, offered us his travel trailer and drove it to Mississippi a few weeks after the storm. In addition, other co-workers from Bethpage, New York, and Dallas, Texas, provisioned the trailer so when Steve delivered it to us, it was stocked with food, cleaning products and necessary camping equipment and supplies. It quickly became home for us and is providing a sense of stability as we recover. Friends at Northrop Grumman are fantastic.

NOTE: We lived in that trailer for a year, sharing a much-crowded campground with many others, including workers there to help with clean-up and rescue.

From Barbara: These many years later, I still have PTSD from this experience, along with anxiety (especially in stormy weather), depression, residual medical issues resulting from being in that contaminated water for so long, and nightmares. These have diminished some, but will never completely disappear from my life.

But God is good – He brought me through that storm for a reason. I am grateful and I thank Him.

Dot Day and Barbara Gaddy

Note: A co-worker noted hers, Jim's, and Daniel's survival of Katrina was a genuine miracle. Standing where they were with the water rising in their house, when it became evident to them that they would have to swim for it against a 90 mph wind to reach safety a quarter mile away, made me appreciate the courage that saved them.

BRUCE GADDY: DEATH DEALER #22 "NINETEEN MINUTES TO LIVE"

Bruce Gaddy as told to Dot Day and Barbara Gaddy

In the 1960s a male high school graduate had several choices: marry and get a job; get a job and wait for his draft lottery number to be called; go to college and wait for his number to be called; or wait at home for the draft/Selective Service letter to appear. Young men were given a random number corresponding to their birthdays. Men with lower numbers were called first and told to report to induction centers where they could be ordered into active duty and possibly sent to the Vietnam War.

To avoid all of that waiting, some young men chose to enlist. Bruce Gaddy chose that route. Looking at him today would not cause one to say he had lived an adventurous life – average height and weight, average appearance, solid citizen, patriotic Christian, fully Southern – all belie his year of active and adventurous duty in Vietnam. His decision to join was impacted by talking to the father of a classmate, Bob Hennington. Bob's father had served in the military, and Bruce was impressed.

Most of the Vietnam-era combat soldiers carried a rucksack and a rifle as they scrambled from a helicopter to an area of engagement to meet Charlie, a member of the Army of the North Vietnam, also known as the Vietcong. Not for Bruce.

Bruce set his sights on becoming a helicopter pilot. Perhaps he had not read the article from a journalist who noted the statistic that a first-time combat helicopter pilot had an average life expectancy of nineteen minutes (*Nineteen Minutes to Live: Helicopter Combat in Vietnam/A Memoir by Lew Jennings.* 2017. Available on Amazon). The statistic might not have deterred him.

Just as a bumblebee does not seem aeronautically equipped to fly, a helicopter looks unable to ascend. But fly they must. As Lew Jennings noted, "There is no such thing as a gliding helicopter ... Unlike the airplane, the helicopter does not want to fly. It is maintained in the air by a variety of forces and controls working in opposition to each other, and if there is any disturbance in the delicate balance, the helicopter stops flying immediately and devastatingly."

In Vietnam, over 12,000 helicopters deployed. They flew over 10 million missions, and 5,806 helicopters were lost (Jennings). The six iconic helicopters deployed in the Vietnam War were the Bell UH-1 Iroquois ("Huey"), the Bell AH-1G Cobra ("Snake"), the Hughes OH-6 Cayuse ("Loach"), the Boeing CH-47 Chinook, the Sikorsky HH3E ("Jolly Green Giant"), and the Sikorsky S-64 Skycrane. Thirty percent of the six types of helicopters lost were Cobras. It was the Cobra that Bruce would be flying.

Bruce's military career began with basic training at Fort Polk, Louisiana. The heat and humidity in the Deep South were good training for Vietnam, not that a young man from Mississippi needed any more instruction. Of that time, Bruce says he had a callus on the end of his index toe (one next to the big toe).

Battles: Glimpses of Truth

He thought he had hit every target put before him in the rifle range examination; he had, but the target he hit was the one put out for the guy beside him. He remembers begging for a passing score.

Basic training is much the same for all enlistees: mud, march, mosquitoes, first aid, general hygiene, teamwork, guns, and more. According to Jennings, most important is "learning to work together, to support each other, to have each other's back regardless of race, creed, color, or religion."

From Fort Polk Bruce went to Fort Rucker, Alabama, about one hundred miles southeast of Montgomery for almost a year of flight school. When the class had almost completed training, he told his Tac Officer he wanted to drop out. The officer talked him out of it, and Bruce stayed in. He described his classmates as throwing him into the Holiday Inn pool in full gear when he survived his first solo, a tradition of the pilots.

On paper the flying process sounds simple, but even learning to fly has dangers, and sometimes the errors end in death for the trainee and his instructor. The training sounds as if the want-to-be pilot should forget everything he had learned about driving a land vehicle. Many of the older generation learned to drive with two primary controls – a simple clutch and manual gear shift. According to Ira McComic *(Notes from a Cobra Pilot in Vietnam-True Tales and Otherwise.* Amirado Publishing. Plano, Texas. 2015.), the helo pilot needed to learn to use many more controls: the right hand controls the *cyclic* – a long stick jutting up from the floor – used to go forward, backward, or sideways; the left hand holds the *collective*, used to go up or down. One end of the collective is the throttle to add or detract gas. This is similar to the gas pedal in a car but is twisted rather than stepped on. If someone has experience with motorcycles, there are similarities, except it's a different hand and is turned in a different direction to go faster or slower.

The pilot cannot move one control at a time; all have to move at the same time because one change affects all the others. Dangers of the helicopter include the possibility of the rotor not being kept at a pretty constant speed for hovering or flying. These spinning blades might fly off if going too fast. If too slow, the blades might have air build under them, pushing the blades up like an umbrella on a windy day. Either of these would crash the helicopter.

In front of the pilot are two footpads to make the nose turn left or right when hovering. The pilot has to learn to suggest rather than demand, or the helicopter becomes unstable.

Bruce stated the hardest part of the preflight training was remembering everything to check, then to look at and know the tolerances of components. For him, the hardest part of flight training was hovering over a certain spot when the instructor handed over the aircraft. The pilot also had to learn autorotation, what to do when the engine fails. Once his flight training was over, the pilot is deemed "fit for flying and dying." Jennings describes a helicopter as "a thousand moving parts that happen to be flying in formation, any one of which can kill you." And many were killed.

The Wall honoring the fallen in Vietnam has some 58,000 names inscribed. Was it their choice to be in a strange and foreign land and to give their lives there? For many, it was not a choice – the draft was in full force. Deferments were possible for some. Some chose to enlist because of a desire to choose a branch of service. If he had not already enlisted or had an earned deferment, once his lottery number was up, he would soon be in Vietnam carrying a rucksack and a rifle.

Jennings recounts the statistics for the helicopter in Vietnam. Helicopters were used to transport soldiers into combat, to bring supplies, to move cargo and equipment, to evacuate the dead and the wounded. Some 12,000+ helicopters would be used in the Vietnam War with over ten million flight hours. Of these, 5,086 helicopters were destroyed; 2,204 pilots killed; and 2,704 crewmembers killed. Helicopter crews accounted for approximately ten percent of all the casualties of this war.

Those men carrying a rucksack and a rifle on the ground saw up to 240 days of combat in a one-year tour. They had casualty rates of four in ten. The motto of flight school "Flying Above the Best" emphasized the focus on those fighting on the ground.

There were three choices for advanced training on the type of helicopter one would fly: the large twin engine, twin rotor Chinook for carrying in supplies and equipment; the Hueys for medevac and troop transport, and the Cobra, a faster gunship for attack and support for the slower-moving transports. The Cobra was Bruce's assignment.

For advanced training, Bruce went to Hunter Army Airfield, associated with Fort Stewart in Savannah, Georgia. He rented a bungalow on the beach for the few weeks of specialized training for flying the Cobra. A portion of the training was learning to use the communication tools, the radios and various frequencies. He had to be able to use the intercom for communication between the pilot and the copilot.

Another part of that training was gunner training.

The Cobra was designed for combat. A loaded Huey cruised at less than 100 knots. A loaded Cobra cruised at 140 knots, about 160 miles per hour. Not only fast, but it was also smooth. It had a stability and control augmentation system designed to help smooth out aircraft motions not due to pilot input, such as wind gusts.

The Cobra has a double bubble canopy; the right side of the cockpit canopy opens for the rear seat pilot; the left side opens for the front seat gunner. The gunner has smaller controls to be able to fly if something renders the pilot unable to fly. Likewise, the pilot has controls for firing the guns. The front seat gunner uses the mini-gun to lay down suppressing fire. The rear-seat commander uses a hot switch control to shoot rockets.

The usual setup for the Cobra is the gunner/copilot in the front seat and the pilot in the rear one. The gunner lays down fire to push the enemy farther away from the landing zone, attacking and killing as many as possible. The job of Cobra pilots was to find, fix, and destroy the enemy while supporting and protecting the troops on the ground. Additionally, the goal was to try not to get killed in the process. The Vietcong put out leaflets dropped to their guerilla fighters warning them not to engage the smaller helicopter, the Cobra. It was okay to approach the larger helicopters. The leaflet advised ARVN soldiers to shoot at the fat helicopters, but to leave the skinny ones alone. The gunship could be easily seen by Charlie unless the pilot was doing low-level flights.

The Vietnam War is known as the "Helicopter War." While helicopters played limited roles in both World War II and the Korean War – mostly for medical evacuation ("medevac") missions – helicopters were involved with nearly every facet of the war in Vietnam: troop transport, scouting, equipment hauling, search and rescue, and providing high-caliber air support for ground troops.

Every branch of the U.S. military employed helicopters in Vietnam. In total, nearly 12,000 helicopters saw action in the war and more than 5,000 were destroyed. "The Army went through helicopters at a ferocious pace during the Vietnam War," says Robert Mitchell, director of the U.S. Army Aviation Museum at Fort Novosel. The young men who flew those helicopters – many of them only 19- or 20-years old – had "absolutely the most dangerous jobs in the war," he adds. For additional information on the helicopters deployed in the Vietnam War, visit https://www.history. com/news/helicopters-vietnam-war

Of the six helicopters from the Vietnam Conflict, the Bell AH-1G Cobra, known as the 'Snake,' is the helicopter Bruce Gaddy flew.

Modified Hueys were effective as gunships, but they weren't built for the job. Back at Bell headquarters, engineers reimagined the Huey as a true fighter aircraft. The result was the Bell AH-1G "Cobra," better known in Vietnam by its nickname, the "Snake."

Battles: Glimpses of Truth

The designation AH stands for "attack helicopter," and the Cobra had the weaponry to back it up. The Cobra was flown by two airmen, like a World War II-era fighter. The pilot sat in the rear and could fire dozens of rockets from wing-mounted launchers. Up front, the co-pilot controlled a rotating "chin turret" armed with a minigun and a grenade launcher.

In an air assault, says Mitchell, the Cobras would race ahead – they could comfortably cruise at 120 knots, almost 140 mph – and lay down cover fire to clear the landing zone for the troop transporters. If a ground commander was taking enemy fire, he would "drop smoke" (a smoke grenade) and call in the Cobras to suppress the threat. The smoke indicated the location of friendly troops.

At the time Bruce was there, the more-than-head-high elephant grass made enemy detection difficult for those troops on the ground.

"You have to know that the ground guys loved the Cobras," says Mitchell.

Gaddy's crew was called on to fly Phantom 3 missions – these missions involved a fire team comprised of two gunships and a command (CNC) helicopter. The command helicopter would pick up an adviser from the target area or village who would provide information to the fire team on the boundaries of the free fire zone. The adviser flew in the helicopter with the CNC pilot not only to help set the boundaries of the free fire zone, but to answer any immediate questions the fire team might have about who or what was included in the free fire zone.

Of the Phantom 3 missions that Gaddy flew he says, "When we went to Bac Lieu and killed a lot of people, we always went on Phantom 3 missions. There was an adviser in the mission area who provided us with the limits on what could be shot in that area. Those areas were considered 'free fire' zones, and we could shoot anything that moved. We had many kills flying these Phantom 3 missions, but one thing I feel I was not aware of is if there were ever any leaflets dropped in these areas to let the people know they were in a 'free fire' zone. Perhaps there had been leaflets dropped in these areas, but at the same time the human beings that we were shooting were considered sympathizers; however, all those sympathizers appeared to me to be rice farmers and everyday people of South Vietnam."

The copilot was outfitted with the gunsight and controls to aim and fire both movable and fixed weapons. These included a Gatling gun or grenade launcher mounted in the turret at the front under the nose of the gunship. The Gatling gun, 44.7' long and 13.5' high, housed in a rotating turret, could fire 3,000 rounds per minute. The 40mm grenade launcher, also in the turret, could fire up to 300 grenades per minute. The Gatling fired 7.6mm rounds at 3,000 per minute. A box of ammo, fed by a chain of linked rounds, was stored in the bay behind the turret, under the front seat position. The box held 3,000 rounds – a maximum of a minute's worth of ammunition.

The grenade launcher threw out 40mm projectiles at a rate of 400 rounds per minute. Its ammo drums, also in the ammo bay, held 400 rounds. These were movable in that they could be pointed at targets by rotating the turret and flexing weapons up or down. The gunner aimed, fired, and adjusted fire by observation of tracer rounds, with every sixth round having a tracer. This gave the effect of looking like a continuous stream of red. The two wing stubs on each side of the fuselage had fixed weapons and carried either rockets or miniguns.

The Cobra's maximum weight was 9.3 thousand pounds, including a crew of two, full ordnance, and full fuel. It used about ten pounds of fuel per minute – two hours of flying with a reserve of 200 pounds. A fuel light would come on when the reserve was reached, indicating there were twenty minutes flying left before running out of fuel. The pilot had to monitor fuel levels as well as navigate and fly. He also fired the weapons in the wing stubs.

Battles: Glimpses of Truth

According to Jennings, the gear of a pilot included a "chicken plate," a heavy bulletproof vest worn over a jungle fatigue shirt. The chicken plate was cinched with a Velcro-strapped survival vest, containing signal flares, signal mirror, first aid kit, strobe light, flashlight, matches, and fishing line. Each had a .38 caliber pistol and a holster that fit onto the belt. The pilot had a helmet strong enough to deflect small arms fire, plus a water jug and a box of C-rations.

"GOOD MORNING, VIETNAM"

Once Bruce completed all phases of flight school, he was commissioned a warrant officer, above the senior-most enlisted ranks. Pledging the same oath as other commissioned officers, he was recognized as a highly skilled, single track specialty officer.

The helicopter squadrons were also tasked to do 'recon' missions. The purpose of these missions included operational and strategic reconnaissance into long-held Vietcong areas and directing air strikes on them. They were also to conduct bomb damage assessment, conduct small-scale reconnaissance and hunter-killer operations, capture and interrogate Viet Cong and North Vietnam Army (VC/NVA) tap communications, bug compounds and offices, rescue downed aircrew and prisoners of war, emplace point minefields and other booby traps, conduct Psychological Operations, and perform counterintelligence operations. North Vietnamese (NVA or PAVN) was the formal army of North Vietnam while the Viet Cong (short for Vietnamese Communist) was the guerrilla army of South Vietnam.

They were to focus on base areas and infiltration routes in the border areas. https://en.wikipedia.org/wiki/Reconnaissance_Projects

United States prisoners of war during the Vietnam War are most known for having used the tap code. It was introduced in June 1965 by four POWs held in the Hỏa Lò ("Hanoi Hilton") prison: Captain Carlyle "Smitty" Harris, one of the POWs, had heard of the tap code being used by prisoners in World War II and remembered a United States Air Force instructor who had discussed it as well.

In Vietnam, the tap code became a very successful way for otherwise isolated prisoners to communicate. POWs would use the tap code in order to communicate to each other between cells in a way which the guards would be unable to pick up on. They used it to communicate everything from what questions interrogators were asking (in order for everyone to stay consistent with a deceptive story), to who was hurt and needed others to donate meager food rations. It was easy to teach, and newly arrived prisoners became fluent in it within a few days. It was even used when prisoners were sitting next to each other but not allowed to talk, by tapping on another's thigh. By overcoming isolation with the tap code, prisoners were said to be able to maintain a chain of command and keep up morale. https://en.wikipedia.org/wiki/Tap_code

Of one of these recon missions, Gaddy remembers, "In February 1970, the U.S. made a big insertion into Cambodia, and my fire team was on standby on the day that the big move into Cambodia occurred. My fire team was called out from Can Tho, my home base, to go into Cambodia to make a recon about 30 miles into Cambodia – specifically a recon of a Cambodian mountain. I had never recon'd a mountain in Cambodia, so I did not know specifically how to complete the mission. I went low-level all the way around the mountain and headed back to friendly surroundings, completing the mission without taking any enemy fire.

"Upon completing that mission, I was told to land my fire team on a soccer field in one of the villages in the area. When we landed there, we were on one side of the soccer field, and there were a lot of ARVANs (Vietnam National Guardsmen) across the soccer field from where we were. As we landed our aircraft, I was looking across the soccer field – and as I got out of my aircraft, I saw the VN soldiers standing around a fire that was on the ground. I walked across the field to see what they were doing, and one soldier had a big, long stick. As I got closer, he saw me looking at the fire wondering what was going on. I discovered they had hay stacked up in a pile that they were burning. He put the long stick under the hay and raised the hay up – and showed me a huge pig they were cooking. It fascinated me that, in the middle of a war zone, they were doing this in such a dangerous situation."

In addition to combat and recon missions, Bruce's fire team was called on to conduct defoliation missions. He describes these "Agent Orange/defoliation" missions – including a bit of 'fun fact' – this way: "We flew defoliation missions with the U.S. Air Force, and in preparation for one of my assigned missions, I had to fly to Saigon to be briefed with the Air Force pilots on how the mission was going to be run. We also received information on the radio frequencies and call signs that we were to use to collaborate to keep each other in sync on what was going on. On the day of the mission, we would be at a specific altitude at a specific time to be able to wait for all the fixed-wing aircraft that would be defoliating the area with the Air Force. One thing I liked about these missions was that we (the Cobra pilots) had to wear gas masks in our aircrafts because the Air Force would be dropping tear gas in the area where the defoliation was being conducted. That made us helicopter pilots sound like 'big dogs' – on the radio – because we sounded like the jet pilots that we were giving cover to.

"We would be at 4,000 feet altitude and whenever the C-123 defoliating aircrafts would start their run, the jet fighters would be giving them gun cover – and as the mission would start, we – the Cobra pilots – would start diving with our aircraft at 4,000 feet trying to keep up with the Air Force fixed wings to give all of them gun cover protection. At the end of the mission of spraying defoliant, the rotary wing helicopter would be down in the Agent Orange or the defoliants that the Air Force would be spraying. At that time, the mission would be over, and we would be able to go back to our home base. However, since we were down in the Agent Orange spray – it would be all over our aircraft. We would have to find a rain cloud to get our aircrafts washed off before returning to base."

Bruce was assigned to the Delta Devils. The Devils had maintenance units and three platoons of pilots. Bruce was in the second platoon, the Death Dealers. The first platoon were the Satans; the third were the Vipers. His call sign was Death Dealer #22.

The Command Tower had a good laugh one day concerning his call sign. He describes it this way. "After completing a mission one day, we were headed back to Can Tho, our home base. Just before landing at Can Tho airfield, I had to radio the tower for clearance to land. When I called the tower for the clearance, I was prepared to give my call sign of 'Death Dealer 22' per protocol – but I got choked on the radio call. Instead of Death Dealer 22, I said 'This is Death Dealer Doo Doo.' I could hear everyone in the tower laughing and carrying on over my misspoken call sign – and the tower responded 'Roger, Death Dealer Doo Doo, you are cleared to land at your company area.' I told the tower, 'Ah, come on guys, I just got choked' – but they had a good laugh about it that day."

A new pilot started off as the gunner in the Cobra's front seat. The front seat pilot was aptly named "Bullet Catcher." He sat at the nose end with plexiglass at his front, overhead and on both sides. It was the best seat for seeing and the best for exposure. He was more at risk than the back-seat pilot. If he survived and qualified, he could then move to the safer second seat, where most of the flying was done. Before going on a mission, the pilot had to update his map books, organize his gear, review his task, and prep his aircraft.

There were other dangers to the pilot in the front seat other than catching bullets. One account that Gaddy reflects on from a mission he flew as the pilot in the front seat provides him confidence in God's watch care over him, even though the experience also left him with a permanent back injury.

He remembers that day like this: "After completing a mission one day I had my fire team to go back to Can Tho. While the team

Battles: Glimpses of Truth

was on the way back to Can Tho, the company called us on the FM radio telling us that we needed to give support to a Charlie Model gunship helicopter that had gone down in an unsecure area. We told them we would and headed to the position to which they had directed us.

"When we got there, we saw a Charlie model gunship Huey helicopter that was sitting in a wilderness area. Captain Parker, the aircraft commander of the helicopter I was in said, 'Let's show them what this Cobra will do.' You can dive a Cobra in steep dives that the ship on the ground could not do. Those guys from the Huey were all out on their aircrafts watching us as we approached them. Captain Parker put our Cobra in a steep dry-gun-run dive on the guys on the ground. Halfway down in this dive, the aircraft veered to the left and we found ourselves flying sideways – until Captain Parker rolled the throttle off. We had begun to auto rotate our aircraft because we had lost the tail rotor and a lot of the drive shaft back to the tail rotor, throwing our center of gravity off in the helicopter.

"When your helicopter begins to auto rotate, you roll the throttle off, disengaging the rotor blades from the turbine engine. When this happens, you bottom out the collective and take the pitch out of the rotor blades, which sets the rotor blades into free-wheeling motion into the wind. Then you rear back on the cyclic to prop back up to at least 500 feet of altitude while descending 500 feet per minute. When you get within around 200 feet above ground you start slowing down on the air speed by rearing back on the cyclic. Eventually, after slowing down the air speed, the aircraft will start falling through toward the ground, and the pilot must start pulling pitch in the rotor blades to allow the aircraft to set down as easy as possible.

"That's the 'normal operation' during an auto-rotation – but in this instance, since we had no tail rotor, we could not pull pitch in the rotor blades to slow the aircraft descent and were forced to

Dot Day and Barbara Gaddy

crash *hard* in a confined wooded area. We hit *hard,* and I can tell you that the hard landing made me get puckered down tight in the front seat trying to stay away from the rotor blades that were still turning quite fast – and could quite possibly cut my head off. Hitting hard will force the rotor blades into the top of the cockpit threatening to cut the front seat pilot's head off in certain situations. After I saw everything was all right, I hollered at Captain Parker to roll the throttle off, but nothing happened! I looked up and he was hauling ass off through the woods! I figured that in that case, I also needed to get out of the aircraft and run for cover. We had landed right beside an old, abandoned rice paddy and that's where I headed to, eventually laying down on an old rice paddy dike to take cover. After listening for any gun shots and finally realizing that there was no enemy gun fire, I took stock of my condition. I looked down at my flight suit and saw that my ankles were the only part of me that were wet from running across the rice paddy.

"So, since there was no gun fire, I stood up and was going to walk back to the aircraft which was about 300 feet back the way I had just come. I took one step off the rice paddy dike, and sank in water up to my neck! I was unable to move from that position because of all the water weeds keeping me from moving. That made me realize that to get across the rice paddy to the point where I was on the rice dike, that I had to have been walking on water – like Jesus Christ did! He was with me that day for sure.

"Since I was stuck in the water and could not move, in a couple of minutes a Huey helicopter flew in and got me out the deep water I was in. I was unable to get up into the aircraft without getting a hand from the door gunner on that ship. When I was finally hoisted into the helicopter, I realized there were no seats – nothing but a vacant cargo area. When the helicopter took off it made a really steep left-hand turn, and I thought I was going to slide out the door because there was nothing to hold on to, but thankfully I managed

Battles: Glimpses of Truth

to hang on inside the Huey. From there the Huey helicopter carried me back to my base in Can Tho."

The 235th Aerial Weapons Company, the Delta Devils, were headquartered at Can Tho; the area of operations was the Delta.

Both the North and South Vietnamese needed the area for its food supply. Farmers there grew two-thirds of all the food in South Vietnam, and three-fourths of the rice. Five-and-one-half million people live in the Mekong Delta of South Vietnam. An aerial view would show meandering rivers, crooked streams, crisscrossing canals, flooded rice paddies, and occasional tree lines. It was made up of mostly rice paddies and mangrove swamps.

Remembering the rice paddies of South Vietnam brings back memories of sampans. Gaddy remembers, "A month or so before I left Vietnam, we were doing missions on the southern tip of Vietnam – the Gulf of Siam back then – we were being told to check out sampans (30- and 40-foot long slender boats) on the very southern tip of Vietnam because most all of them were considered Viet Cong, the enemy. Several times we fired upon these sampans and found just how hard it is to hit a boat this size out in the expanse of flat water. It's hard to hit a boat when you have no visual reference. We were doing that when I left Vietnam and learned later that the Viet Cong enemy were saying that we were shooting up friendly boats. This became a major consideration after I left the country."

The pilots stayed in hooches with plywood walls, cots, and metal lockers. Lew Jennings noted a strange pungent odor – "smell of burning feces excreted by thousands of military personnel, soaked in fuel oil and set afire." It was a daily regimen at every military base. Troops were issued pills to fight off malaria and salt pills to stay hydrated.

Career Stats and Achievements

Of Bruce Gaddy's deployment, he states, "During the year I was there, I had over 209 confirmed kills and no telling how many non-confirmed because we did a lot of shooting, giving ground troops cover.

"My company was an armed helicopter company based at Can Tho, Vietnam, to give anybody that needed protection or guns that support. They could call on us to give them help of whatever kind they needed. One time we were called out to an area close to the Cambodian border – to support a Navy PT boat that was up a small canal. They needed help because they were under heavy fire. When we arrived, it was close to dark. At the time we were only armed with Flechette rockets – rockets with 4,000 nails in each rocket. I had radio contact with the Navy PT boat that was on the canal. He said he was under heavy fire and needed some relief. I told him I only had the Flechette rockets and had no control over what area they would strike – and that he needed to get under something for protection. He did so and told me he was ready for the relief. We rolled in and shot the area as much as possible, unloaded our armaments on this area. After I'd unloaded the rockets, I called him back – and he said he was not taking any more fire and he released us to go back to our home base. Mission accomplished!"

Bruce came out of the military having earned thirty-six air medals, each representing twenty-five hours of combat flight. In over nine hundred hours of combat flying time, he also was awarded two Bronze Stars, given for "meritorious achievement in ground operations against hostile forces."

Bruce is also the recipient of the Distinguished Flying Cross for "heroism while participating in aerial fight."

Until 2024, he was unsure of the specific events that effected these awards.

Battles: Glimpses of Truth

When a cousin of Bruce's was going through her mother's effects following her mother's death, she came across two letters that Gaddy had written to her mother, Linda Hall, while he was in Vietnam. In one of the letters he writes,

"Dear Linda, I want to thank you for writing. I haven't received a letter from anyone in Crystal Springs (Mississippi) in about 3 weeks or more. Just to hear about places getting robbed in Crystal Springs means a lot right now.

"Everyday I wait for mail call and then when it comes there isn't a thing for me. Bigmama use to send me the Meteor (the local newspaper) but I haven't received one of those for over a month. You know it really lets your morale drop when you don't receive any letters from home. You also find out who your friends are. So I want to thank you for writing me."

The second letter to Linda begins, "Dear Linda, I hope this letter finds you and the girls in good health. I'm doing OK myself. I've had 2 or 3 close calls since I've been here but I'm doing fine."

Included in the envelope that Yvonne, Bruce's cousin, gave to him was the write-up from The Meteor that provided the details of his receiving the Distinguished Flying Cross. The article recounts the award and experience as follows:

"Bruce Gaddy Gets Commendation"

"Warrant Officer 1 Billy B Gaddy of Crystal Springs has been awarded the distinguished flying cross for heroism in the Republic of Vietnam on March 3, 1970. The citation reads as follows:

"For heroism while participating in aerial flight evidenced by voluntary actions above and beyond the call of duty: these men distinguished themselves by exceptionally valorous actions while serving as pilots in command of two ships in a fire team of three attack helicopters in support of friendly ground forces. As the first

Dot Day and Barbara Gaddy

troop carrying helicopter touched down, it was met by a hail of enemy automatic weapons fire and one aircraft was shot down. The fire team immediately attacked the heavily fortified enemy positions, and these men braved a tremendous volume of fire to provide protection for the troop carrying aircraft. Throughout the day they flew between the enemy and the ground troops to provide the needed fire support. By this time their ships had suffered heavy battle damage, but through their professional ability they were able to get the crippled aircraft back to Binh Thuy. Throughout the day, these men displayed exceptional courage and valor by repeatedly exposing themselves in hostile fire in order to protect the lives of others. Their actions were in keeping with the highest traditions of the military service and reflect great credit upon themselves, their unit, and the United States Army."

During Gaddy's recounting of events during his tour in Vietnam, there were several times he paused mid-sentence and said in a contemplative voice, "No, I'm not going there," or "That's enough on that one," letting me know that the remaining events of the story were not forthcoming. The traumatic events of war – the "war is hell" events – the PTSD-causing events – would remain with him and on those battlefields.

Haunting memories and nightmares came home with Bruce Gaddy.

MAUDIE
Dr. Bob Rich

The little darling of my heart is not pretty, no. I have read about Dr. Down's work, and he calls her kind Mongoloid; but I went to the library and found pictures of Mongolian people, and actually she doesn't look like them.

Although she is seven years old, she cannot speak, and I have not been able to toilet train her, but neither of these matters. She is pure joy in my life, and my life wraps around her, though I do wonder what will happen to her when she is grown and I am gone.

Craig ran off as soon as he found out he had a handicapped child, and now has a couple of tantrum-throwing, bickering sons with that Jane floozy, and serve him right. He hasn't paid me a penny since, but at least the house is mine, and his parents do help, and told me they shall leave me what they have when they die. And as a seamstress, I can earn a living from home. When I have no orders for ball- or wedding-dresses, I take in mending.

Today being a fine, sunny day, mid-morning I tied a bonnet on Maudie's head and one on mine and took her on a stroll to the park. I do need to keep a tight hold of her hand because she has no more sense of safety than a puppy. Once, she let go of my hand and ran right under a horse! The animal reared, nearly upsetting the

Dot Day and Barbara Gaddy

carriage, and it was only the grace of God that saved my Maudie from being trampled.

But today, the busy road was safe from her impulsiveness. We arrived at the park without mishap, but there a bearded man stood with a lead in his hand, and a dog running around. It was of the breed I believe is called a bull mastiff. Upon seeing us, his owner whistled, but instead of going to him, the dog approached us, tail wagging. Maudie sprang forward and hugged the beast around the neck and my heart near-stopped from fright, but the only untoward reaction was a big pink tongue licking her ear. Heaven be praised, a wash will correct the effects.

Also looking relieved, the man smiled at me and strode over to the duo. He gently stroked Maudie's hair, and she looked up at him with a serious gaze; then she surprised me once more. She held her arms up to him as she frequently does to me. He bent with grace and lifted her into a hug. Never have I known her to do this to a stranger; indeed, she tends to be shy, and no wonder with all the disdain directed upon her.

Over her dark hair, he smiled at me. "Ma'am," he said, "your little daughter has a certain genius."

"Kind of you, sir, but fate has been unkind to her with regard to intelligence. She has not even mastered the ability to speak."

"Yes, but she has the genius of love. She can clearly sense the inner, hidden emotions and responds to them with the directness of instinct. Oh, I'd better introduce myself. I am Tavis McPherson."

"I am Kate Wiley, and your new friend is Maudie Wiley."

"And my friend, and sadly, only companion is Conan. Six months ago, my wife died in childbirth." Though his face stayed calm, though he continued to hold my little girl with affection, I saw he was close to crying. Also, it was remarkable and against custom for him to disclose his tragedy to a complete stranger.

Battles: Glimpses of Truth

He put Maudie down, took a small ball from a pocket and threw it. Conan raced to fetch it back; and, giggling, Maudie ran after him.

He turned back to me. "Mrs. Wiley, I don't believe in coincidence. The four of us are here in this park, with no others, because we were meant to meet."

Conan was back in a flash but dropped the ball in front of Maudie rather than his owner. When she looked on without comprehension, Mr. McPherson picked up the ball, put it in her hand and threw it with her. While it only went a short distance and the dog fetched it back immediately, they repeated the action several times. Then, to my amazement, Maudie threw the ball unsupported.

Mr. McPherson turned to me. "You see, Mrs. Wiley, she is capable of learning. Perhaps we can teach her to speak after all, although surely you and your husband have tried many methods." Then he looked at my face. "Oh. I see. You're alone."

What an exceptional man! I was struck for words and could do no more than smile at him.

"Ma'am," he said, "I feel sorry for the fellow, for he has deprived himself of the opportunity to benefit from Maudie's inexhaustible fount of love, and ... if I may say so, of the company of a lovely wife."

I felt my face flush. When I look in the mirror, the woman I see is not at all lovely.

Seeing no further action, Conan curled up at his owner's feet. Maudie hugged him once more. Mr. McPherson looked down, then gently stirred the dog with a foot. "Hey, we're here to provide you with exercise," he said as he bent, then threw the ball again. "I find a great deal of consolation from the love of Jesus, for I am in His service, the humble minister of New Hope, just around the corner."

I knew the church to be Presbyterian. Though I was raised in the Church of England, I have not attended services since Craig's departure. Maudie was typically not well received by many in the

93

Dot Day and Barbara Gaddy

congregation, and I had no one locally I would trust to mind her. I explained this to Mr. McPherson.

"Oh, ma'am, you have just provided the inspiration for my sermon next Sunday," he said. "Would you be so kind as to bring Maudie to the service at 10 o'clock? I guarantee kindness from all."

So, on Sunday morning, I ensured Maudie smelt sweet and both of us looked neat, and with some trepidation walked to church. As I entered the alcove, a grandmotherly woman approached. "You must be Mrs. Wiley," she said with a smile. "The reverend appointed me to welcome you and care for your little daughter's welfare. I am Mrs. Hosberger."

"Thank you, ma'am, you're most kind."

Looking down on Maudie, she said, "My first child was also ... very different. He died at only fifteen years of age, but he taught me the lesson of compassion for all."

She escorted me to a large room full of people chatting in groups, holding small plates of food and steaming cups. Maudie was instantly terrified, of course, and hugged my leg, pushing her face against me. I managed to gently prise her loose and lifted her, so it was against my shoulder that she hid.

Mrs. Hosberger took me first to a side table and used sweetmeats to induce Maudie to lose her terror. Then we went from group to group. She introduced me, though it was impossible for me to remember the many names. Her invariable statement was, "Allow me to introduce Mrs. Wiley and her darling daughter, whom God has sent along for us to cherish."

Many indeed responded with a genuine smile, and the others at least hid their disdain.

A bell rang, and everyone proceeded into the church proper. Mrs. Hosberger directed us to sit in the front row and would not allow otherwise.

Battles: Glimpses of Truth

The service was not too different from my memory of it. Mr. McPherson chose St. Paul's beautiful words on love in I Corinthians 13, and then expanded upon it.

"This is central to Jesus' message. Does He not say in Matthew 5:44 that we should love even those who do us harm? It is easy to love those who love you, to care for those who care for you, to do good to those who do you good. It's even a sort of a selfishness. But to love all of God's creations, without limit, without regard to what they do or fail to do, requires a kind of a genius. Oh, all of us need to try to remember to replace hate and fear with love. But for some exceptional people, this comes naturally. This past week, it has been my pleasure to meet such a genius of love. Mrs. Wiley, would you be so kind as to bring Maudie here?"

Flustered, I couldn't move for a moment, but Mrs. Hosberger gave me a little friendly nudge. I stood with Maudie still in my arms, and advanced to stand beside Mr. McPherson.

"This little child was born into a body most consider to be damaged, faulty, to be shunned and hidden away. But she has also been blessed with this genius of love I have mentioned. Instinctively, without having been taught, she senses love, and returns it without limit. Watch." He gently took hold of Maudie's head, naturally pressed against my shoulder, and turned her to look at him.

Their eyes locked, then she turned, and as in the park, she held out her arms to him, leaning away from me.

I passed her over, and she hugged his neck, to a susurration of comment from the congregation.

The minister looked at them over her head. "All living beings are God's creations. All have God's love, and spreading that love to all is performing God's command. This little child is our teacher." With a smile he handed Maudie back to me and signaled with his eyes for me to return to my seat.

Dot Day and Barbara Gaddy

A little later, as the ceremony drew to a close, I asked Mrs. Hosberger, "Since his personal tragedy, how does Mr. McPherson cope with the tasks of everyday life?"

While standing up, she replied, "We have a roster of families who invite him to luncheon and dinner and look after other domestic tasks. Being the kind of person he is, he continues to complain, saying he doesn't wish to be a load on others, but ... ."

"I should think it a privilege rather than a load," I said, standing also. "It would be my great pleasure to join in. Being a seamstress, perhaps I can care for his clothes?"

We joined the line waiting to exit. She said, "That would be most appreciated; and as I understand it, you're without a husband, so it would not very well be proper to have him visit you for meals."

I could smell the need to clean Maudie up, and upon my request, Mrs. Hosberger directed me to a side room, which was an indoor privy, with a bucket of water for washing one's hands. I managed to fix the problem in a few minutes, then returned to the foyer. Most people were gone, but Mrs. Hosberger waited for me with three other ladies. She had informed them of my profession, and we arranged that a Mrs. Bartley would take me to the manse Monday morning so I could inspect the reverend's clothing and take away any needing repair. Another lady, Mrs. Strand, said, "Oh, my daughter has just become betrothed. Do you have any samples of wedding gowns?"

So, while of course we could not transact business on a Sunday, I knew that my drawings and four copies of photographic pictures from past clients would gain her approval.

When Maudie and I arrived at the manse on Monday, Mrs. Bartley and Mrs. Hosberger awaited us. "I wish to try what the reverend showed us," Mrs. Hosberger said. She squatted and held her arms out. Maudie looked at her with serious eyes for a long moment – then ran forward into a hug. The lady stood, holding her.

Amazing, truly.

Battles: Glimpses of Truth

Within half an hour, we collected a basketful of mending, which I took home, Maudie walking between the two women, each holding one of her hands. Then Mrs. Bartley left us.

Mrs. Hosberger said, "I shall try on Maudie what worked with my poor Edward." She picked Maudie up and sat, settling Maudie on her lap so they were face to face. She tickled the child's nose with a finger, saying "Nose." Maudie of course laughed without comprehension. Mrs. Hosberger then touched her own nose, repeating, "Nose," and alternated the two actions over and over while I busied myself replacing the reverend's missing buttons and darning his socks. After many repetitions, the lady took Maudie's hand and used her tiny finger for the nose pointings.

I needed to go into another room to use my Singer sewing machine to repair a loose seam. When I returned, Mrs. Hosberger handed Maudie to me.

A slim finger touched my nose, and Maudie clearly said, "Nose!" the first word of the seven years of her life.

COMMERCIALS, TV & OLD AGE

Hazel Lonie

Bewitched was funny – when I was younger. *Yancy Derringer* was entertaining – now I see the very handsome Pahoo being called a savage and treated less than human. Tonto, I've learned, means fool. Westerns, well, I still watch some of them – *Rawhide*, *Gunsmoke*, *Bonanza*, and *The Rifleman* – I loved the sound of Mark's voice on that show. Could that show work as well if Mark McCain had been female instead? Think of all the taboo story lines as Markesha would venture into puberty. No matter, the indigenous people were being stripped of their land and being portrayed as wild ungodly savages for trying to keep what was rightfully theirs.

How can they be called illegals today when they were taken from their land and sent to reservations or further south into Central and South America? "Remember the Alamo"?

I loved *Amos & Andy*. Timmy Martin, Joey with Fury and Dennis Mitchell, the male leads, had fine adventure shows, and I never questioned any of it. After all, boys must be seen as smarter; even Lucy, the American red-headed white woman, was over-shadowed by a Cuban funny-talking male. Fred Mertz and Ricky Ricardo, Ward Cleaver and Jim Anderson ruled the roosts; and later Cliff Huxtable knew better than Clair, a practicing attorney, as they headed their households.

Put my ignorance aside – true I missed the bigotry of television as a child. Lately though, shows like *Jane the Virgin* and *Lucifer* are so disturbing I haven't tried to watch them. Don't even think of all the demons, zombies and other ungodly mess being fed to today's youth. Yet we wonder why the young ones are so unstable. It took me several times before I realized that Miss 2-0-2-0 was happy about her match to a red, naked Satan. The frail little white girl who's afraid of Hispanic and Black men is right at home with Satan? He's huge in stature with enormous horns, but she smiles and doesn't show fear. Once there was an uproar because of an interracial couple in a Cheerios commercial. WTH has happened?

AWAKENING TO GOD'S LOVE

Cindy Mount

It seems strange to be offering my life story to the world. Over 40 years in the making condensed into a few short paragraphs. I have often wondered if people ever consider the story behind the story. This story is satisfying and uplifting but contains so much that is not said. Tears, frustrations, anger, bitterness, and unforgiveness that have finally given way to mercy and new life are testimony to what only God can accomplish in people.

Praise God for His infinite mercy!

On that day, the deaf will hear the words from a book. And out of their gloom and darkness, the eyes of those who are blind will see. The humble will be filled with fresh joy from the LORD, and they will rejoice in the Holy One of Israel. Isaiah 29:18-19 NASB, VOICE, NLT, ICB

My mind is filled with various thoughts this morning. I have been reflecting on conversations and comments I have read in articles or blog posts. Here is my attempt to put it into words.

Westminster Catechism: What is the chief end of man?
Man's chief end is to glorify God and to enjoy Him forever.

During a conversation, a friend shared this timeless truth from the Westminster Catechism, when I shared how much I had been enjoying God. Though unfamiliar with it, I fully agreed with its truth. Again, this statement appeared in a devotional today, prompting me to look it up and read it myself. A dawning realization came to me. I learned this truth from Abba, not knowing the Westminster Catechism – to love and worship Him wholeheartedly in everything I do. This realization humbled me, and I have yet to comprehend it fully.

In what ways does worship manifest itself in daily life? The presence of God makes ordinary faithfulness extraordinary. Anyone willing to focus and prioritize Him over his sense of self, feelings, or desires can accomplish this.

I will bless the LORD who guides me; even at night, my heart instructs me. I will bless the Eternal, whose wise teaching orchestrates my days and centers my mind at night. I know the LORD is always with me. I will not be shaken. I will not live in fear or abandon my calling. I will always let the LORD guide me because He stands at my right hand. Psalm 16:77-8 NLT, VOICE, CSB

"LORD, You alone are my portion and cup; You secure my lot. The boundary lines have fallen for me in pleasant places; surely, I have a delightful inheritance. Psalm 16:5 NIV

My response: *Because You are in them!*

Battles: Glimpses of Truth

Watching my husband recover from his motorcycle accident and observing his awakening to God's love reminds me of my own long ago. Even after all this time, it will take a lifetime to grasp the fullness of His love. Initially spoken about the people of Israel, the words in Isaiah are relevant to any who do not know the Lord in our present day. Broken by sin, shame, and what the world has provided, we have been blind to His presence in our lives and His love for us.

Similar to waking up from a long, deep sleep, waking up to the reality of God's love can be disorienting, overwhelming, and confusing. Since we have never known or been able to receive God's pure unconditional love before, it can be intoxicating once we believe Him. His love changes everything! Our vision and hearing begin to gain clarity and understanding. God's refining merciful love opens windows, then doors to experience life in a whole new way than we have ever known, full of His promise to be with us in all that life offers.

Now, I observe my husband, a man who never cried openly, weep with tears as he recalls the ways God has loved him all along, but he could never see or receive. I have experienced this joy, too. This is the first time I can share it with my husband. God's love is excellent, and only He has the power to transform hearts and lives.

Have you ever experienced God's love for you? Do you believe He loves you personally? Could you ask Him and see how He responds? He loves us more than we can imagine. His Word says so.

Wake up, sleeper, rise from the dead, and Christ will shine on you. Ephesians 5:14 NIV

Jesus, You are truly superb and awe-inspiring! Your promises of unfailing love never fail to come to fruition. May Your magnificence be apparent in our lives and Your glory be evident in our

Dot Day and Barbara Gaddy

world so that we may witness Your power and majesty. You alone are worthy of all the blessings, honor, and praise!

We present our requests to You. We trust You know what is best for us. Will You answer and guide us in ways that surpass our understanding? As we learn to abide in You, provide for our needs, even our desires. Fulfill Your purpose in every situation and request. We pray for peace in Jerusalem and Israel and ask for supernatural wisdom, discernment, and protection for their leaders and vulnerable people. You alone are Commander of Heaven's armies! All eyes are on You for what is needed. All glory, honor, and praise to You! Lord of Hosts!

May we shout for joy when we hear of Your victory and raise a banner in the name of God. Psalm 20:5 NLT

TOPGUN:
STEVE SPRAGG'S STORY
Dot Day

If you were to ask a Navy pilot who was the better pilot, a naval aviator or an Air Force pilot, he would answer without hesitation, "The Navy pilot." If you then asked an Air Force aviator the same question, he might sheepishly hesitate before answering, "The Navy pilot." He would go on to explain the Air Force pilot lands on a runway on the ground, but a Navy pilot has to land on an aircraft carrier, hoping to be stopped by a tailhook wire. Frequently he is called to land at night. The best of the naval aviators are TopGuns. Steve Spragg's story as a TopGun started at a young age.

In his poem "Harlem," the poet Langston Hughes asked the question, "What happens to a dream deferred?" Five-year-old Steve Spragg went to a Little Rock runway to watch a B-58, a 4-engine supersonic bomber, take off. This event with his Air Force dad led him to develop a love for aviation and a desire to be a pilot. However, this dream was not to be realized. Around the age of 12, it crashed. Steve began wearing glasses; pilots need perfect vision. Although flying would not be his career path, he continued to be somewhat obsessed with the F-14.

The Navy's F-14, also known as the Tomcat, was the jet fighter featured in the 1986 movie *Top Gun*. First used in the last days of the Vietnam War to fly air patrol missions, they designed it in the 1960s with the aerodynamic and electronic capacities to defend U.S. aircraft – carrier operations at long ranges against Soviet aircraft and missiles. The F-14 was in active service from 1972 to 2006. "In 1981, carrier-based F-14s directly engaged Libyan fighters in air-to-air combat: in 1986 they flew combat air patrol during bombing operations against that country." ("F-14: Introduction and Quick Facts." Editors of *Encyclopedia Britannica* Internet accessed 01 Nov. 2021.)

The *Encyclopedia Britannica* notes the F-14 could "surpass Mach 2 (twice the speed of sound) at high altitudes and Mach 1 at sea level." It could engage other jets in air-to-air combat as well as carrying out bombing missions. "In 1995, during NATO's intervention in Bosnia, given the nickname 'Bombcats' F-14s struck targets with laser-guided bombs."

When there have been no other alternatives, the Navy has gone to war by sea, air, and land to defend its interests in the Middle East, Southwest Asia, and Eastern Africa. The Navy also operates peacefully in the areas of humanitarian assistance, maritime rescue, and military exercises with regional allies.

Twenty-seven countries and three critical points are in the Fifth Fleet area, particularly the Strait of Hormuz, the Suez Canal, and the Bab al-Mandeb at the southern tip of Yemen. "The Navy owes its success in this region to the patriotism, professionalism, pride, hard work, and self-sacrifice of the officers and enlisted men and women assigned to U. S. Naval Forces Central Command/5th fleet." (Britannica, The Editors of Encyclopaedia. "F-14." *Encyclopedia Britannica*, 11 Jan. 2018, https://www.britannica.com/technology/F-14. Accessed 1 November 2021.)

Although he was in college, Steve was not quite content with his course of study and began talking with a recruiter who asked him if he could be interested in flying in the rear seat of an F-14. This suggestion altered his career path; he worked to become a RIO in an F-14 fighter jet. His 20th birthday was August 1, 1979, and he signed with the Navy four days prior to turning twenty.

The pilot occupies the front seat of a Tomcat; the rear seat is the domain of the radar intercept officer, the RIO. Steve would work toward a career that required him to monitor the weapon system, capable of tracking up to 24 enemy aircraft as far away as 195 miles while simultaneously guiding long-range missiles to six of them. "Medium- and short-range missiles could also be carried under the inner wings and fuselage, as could bombs for attacking surface targets. A 20-millimetre rotary cannon was mounted in the fuselage for close-range dogfighting." (*Encyclopedia Britannica.*)

RIOs "were the backseaters who operated the F-14's weapon system, responsible for communication and navigation and performed other aircraft duties. During a radar intercept, the RIO directed the pilot, so he was 'verbally flying' the aircraft. A normal mission for any fighter aircraft is to intercept an airborne target. To intercept it, it is necessary to find it on the radar. Then calculations must be made by someone who has the best angle to intercept the target using radar and to get in the firing position. That someone is the radar intercept officer." (Baranek, Dave "Bio." "Did the F-14 Tomcat have Flight Controls in the Rear cockpit?" in Fight's On! 21 July 2020. accessed 13 June 2022.) {NOTE: Interested readers may want to visit www.TopgunBio.com for Dave Baranek's reprint of a magazine article from *California* by author Ehud Yonay.}

Steve noted another role, "My role was to act as a co-pilot during the landing and takeoff phases of flight whether flying from land or an aircraft carrier. I would monitor all flight instruments and assist the pilot as needed. Different pilots had different preferences, so it was always important to brief and discuss their particular needs before each flight with a new pilot."

Dot Day and Barbara Gaddy

When Steve signed with the Navy, he contracted to attend AVROC – Aviation Reserve Officer Candidate School in Pensacola, Florida. Steve spent the summer of 1980, his junior year summer, in Pensacola – eight weeks of the hottest summer on record. They suffered from heat and oppressive humidity, and their training made no allowances for discomfort. While the academics concerned both naval and Marine Corps materials, they went through full military training with a Marine drill sergeant as the instructor. Steve affirmed that he was "Navy owned and Marine trained."

In Memphis his major was sociology with emphases in human resources and business. He graduated from Memphis State December 1981. By February 1982 he was fully Navy.

He was commissioned an ensign April 30, 1982, and began flight school in Pensacola. The first phase was basic and intermediate instruction, VT-10 (VT designates a training squadron.). Following that, Steve was selected for advanced training, VT-86. This training built on the earlier training with additional emphasis on systems, instrument and radar navigation, radar intercept and attack, high-speed low-level flight, advanced aerial combat maneuvering and advanced communications" ("VT-86." *Wikipedia* Foundation. *Wikipedia – Academic Dictionaries and Encyclopedias*, 2010. Accessed 16 April 2022.)

Steve mentioned the use of virtual simulation in his training: "Simulators allowed aircrews to work through stressful emergency situations in a safe environment. This repetition aimed at making many of those required actions a 'muscle memory' reaction to an actual emergency. I know it made actual emergencies less stressful for me. One friend had to eject and had no recall of any events between ejection and stepping off the rescue helicopter on the deck of the aircraft carrier even though he had performed a number of emergency procedures in between." He stated the simulation was not as realistic in the 1980s as it is now. The dome simulator at that time allowed only a 90-degree field of vision.

Battles: Glimpses of Truth

In addition to simulation, the air crews trained in a variety of aircraft. Further training would prepare them for the actual type assigned to them.

Steve earned his wings May 13, 1983, graduating third in his class. Because of his stellar performance he was allowed to choose his place of assignment on the East Coast or the West Coast or Japan. Steve chose Miramar, San Diego. His assigned squad was VF-124 (VF designates a fighting squadron.) for training in the F-14. He reported there in August 1983. When that schooling was complete, he was assigned to VF-154, the Black Knights, a naval strike fighter squadron.

Spragg joined the Black Knights for two deployments in 1985 and 1987 flying off the *USS Constellation* (C V-64), a non-nuclear aircraft carrier called "America's flagship" by President Ronald Reagan. Steve explained the practice of pairing pilot and RIO: "Usually a junior RIO was first assigned to a more experienced pilot for their first cruise. After gaining experience (flight hours in the F-14) pilots/RIOs with similar experience (250-500 hours) were then crewed together.

"After gaining even more experience, those experienced RIOs were assigned to fly with less experienced pilots. For my second cruise, I was crewed with a new pilot who had just reported to our squadron a few days before we deployed. Crews that were paired together usually flew together as much as possible for a period of time (four-six months) or for a specific training evolution – missile shoots, carrier qualifications, etc."

Most, if not all, aircraft crews want the opportunity to advance their skills. The Navy offers this opportunity to a select few with the TopGun's Weapons Fighter School. In the closing days of the Vietnam War, there was concern that the greatly expensive Tomcat was not as successful as the brass needed it to be. They commissioned Frank Ault to determine causes. He and a group of experts pored over the mechanics, the weaponry, the human element. The

Dot Day and Barbara Gaddy

Air Force believed there were flaws in the machinery and technology and worked in those areas. On the other hand, the Navy set to work on the techniques and maneuvers of their pilots. The result was TopGun schooling where the best teachers trained the most elite pilots and RIOs.

TopGun became a reality thanks to Ault and company. Only months after publication of the Ault Report, Naval Air Station Miramar established TopGun and graduated the first class the same year. The program known as TopGun was commissioned as a squadron, the Navy Fighter Weapons School, in 1972. TopGun is now physically located at the Naval Air Station Fallon in Nevada, though it was previously housed at Miramar. One writer explained "only the top one percent of Navy pilots are permitted to train in the program" (https://veteran.com>topgunschool).

These handpicked students are described as hardworking, humble, and approachable. The leaders do not want anyone who has a big ego, a death wish, or believes he has made it and no one else could be as good as he is. A mother of a TopGun pilot states, "They are also cocky, demonstrating their confidence in their abilities." Spragg discussed his cohorts, "We all laughed at one another and sometimes laughed at ourselves. To be certain, if one ever did anything stupid/questionable on the ground or in the air, one's squadron mates certainly let them know about it with no small amount of laughing and/or ridicule. It was an accepted part of life in the super-competitive environment of a U. S. Navy fighter squadron."

This schooling includes dogfights that pit the trainees against the trainers. Once this schooling has been completed, students have the assignment of training other pilots in these maneuvers. A commanding officer can recommend a crew approximately every 18 months to attend the school. It is a signal honor to be deemed worthy of this training and then be tasked with passing on the expertise to other crews in one's squadron.

Battles: Glimpses of Truth

One of Steve's roles as a RIO was to pull the lever to eject both the pilot and himself in case the pilot did not recognize the danger of continuing attempts to control the aircraft past its and/or his capability. The handles for ejection were located above his head and between his legs. He could choose to use either one. Steve almost reached for the control four times in his aviation career.

After his training and deployment, he returned to Pensacola as an instructor for the advanced stage of simulator training (VT-84) and to serve as a mentor for one of the trainees. During his stint there, he escorted a space shuttle pilot around the site. He asked him the hardest thing he had to do as a pilot. His answer was "land on an aircraft carrier at night." Steve laughed telling this, expecting to hear something other than a task Navy aviators did routinely.

When Steve left active duty, he joined a reserve unit. He notes serving in four units, 1990-1995, two of them based in Dallas. He was called to active duty for Operation Delta Storm in 1992 with the fighter squadron VF-201, the Hunters, Joint Air Force Southwest Asia or JTFSWA. In 1993 he deployed three months to Saudi Arabia, technically serving in combat.

He said, "I can say that I did not enjoy some of the administrative parts of my job – what are called 'collateral' duties. Probably the toughest lessons learned were the ones where you were killed (simulated) in a training evolution/mock battle. That taught us that we were not invincible and that there was always something to learn or a skill that needed to be practiced more."

"There was really no worst part as it came to flying. If I had to pick a worst part, I would have to say it would be losing so many of my friends to F-14 mishaps – I personally lost six friends in F-14s."

TO JOHN UPON HIS RETURN

Carol Ashley

(Used by poet's permission from *Bonus Addition)*

Welcome back from Iraq!
Three tours are quite enough,
So I called in the family!
They're bringing lots of stuff.
Dear Martha's bringing masking tape,
And Jerrell's got the rope.
While Bobbie has a lock and chain,
Miss Linda nails, I hope,
And me, I've got a staple gun
In case you want to roam.
I am prepared to use them all
To keep your butt at home!

STOIC PATRIOT: BILL DAY

Dorothy A. Day

"If I make it, I make it; if not, then not. There's nothing I can do about it." Having recently turned 22, Bill Day accepted his life was in God's hands. Bill's plane completed its bombing mission and was shot down 13 April 1944, and he became a prisoner of war in World War II, first in Hungary, then in Poland. He was taken captive by Hungarians, whisked away to a hospital in Budapest where he received treatment for 70 days. He was then taken to a federal prison there for the next 25 days. After a train ride through the country to the inside of Germany, he arrived at Stalag Luft III on 23 July 1944. He remained there through January 1945 when he began his repatriation process.

> Mission number 24, 13 April 1944. At 0950 hours 24 aircraft took off to bomb Budapest/Tokol A/D, Hungary. Four aircraft returned early. 20 aircraft dropped 384 x 120 pounds (23.04 tons) Frags instantaneous fuse bombs on primary target at 12:53 hours from 22,800'. Two of the above aircraft returned six clusters to base. 16 aircraft returned at 1530 hrs. for our aircraft lost in the vicinity of rally point. One aircraft lost when landing at homebase because the tire blew out. 16 FW 190s were over the formation at the

Dot Day and Barbara Gaddy

IP but did not attack. 30–36 E/A Me109s, Fw 190s, Me 110s, and Me 210s attacked aggressively after bombs way from 1250 to 1320 hours. Five Me 110s in line abreast, firing rocMe109 with two wing tanks one Me210 with belly tanks were observed. Flak was moderate, accurate, heavy. Bombs covered the airdrome and hangars. (Report from the War Department, Judge Advocate General, for Claims Division.)

William Thomas Day was born 22 February 1922 in Greensboro, Alabama; he was the younger of two children. His father was William Tennison Day, and his mother was Frankie Smith Day from Yazoo County, Mississippi. Frankie left her home in Mississippi to go to Alabama as a schoolteacher in a one-room school. There she met Tennison, a tall, handsome farmer and WWI veteran of the Linden, Alabama, area. Tennison was the only Day born to his mother. He lost his father in a lumbering accident, and she remarried an Anderson. Tennison had several Anderson half siblings. I can imagine the tall stocky farmer becoming quite unpopular in Greensboro, Alabama, and the surrounding area when he took the slim schoolteacher away from her classroom. The couple had two children, William Thomas and Katherine.

Bill graduated from Greensboro High School after completing his 12 years of schooling. He sounded like a typical high school athlete of that era, playing both baseball and football. He was a left-handed pitcher for the high school team and had the possibility of playing at a higher level. When he cut his finger on his left hand while working at a sawmill, he was certain his pitching would not be good enough to play pro baseball, and he gave up the dream of being a southpaw starter. Semi-pro baseball didn't pay enough to support a family.

The family moved to Yazoo County after his graduation. He worked as a store clerk at a pharmacy until he decided to enlist on

Battles: Glimpses of Truth

31 October 1942. He gave his home address as Satartia, Mississippi, when he was inducted in Yazoo City, Mississippi.

When Day joined the Army Air Corps, he received his basic training at what became Keesler Air Force Base in Biloxi, Mississippi; then he went on to San Antonio, Texas, for six weeks of aerial gunnery school at the base later called Lackland Air Force Base. Following that, his next assignment was 19 weeks at McCook Airbase in McCook, Nebraska, training as an airplane mechanic.

His training also included detail stripping of the gun, blind-folded, after the instructor had mixed up the parts; then when reassembling the gun, the trainee had to pick up and name the part and describe what was broken with two or three additional parts tossed in by the instructor. He also had to show ability to estimate range at 300 yards, 600 yards, and 1,000 yards for enemy aircraft. Ninety-five percent of the Army Air Corps trainees completed the training phase of the program without injury. They won the safety award of the National Safety Council because of their record (*Air Force: Official Journal of the US Army Air Forces*. July 1943. Volume 26 Number 7.).

The Nebraska plains were ideally suited for an airbase training area. Where corn and winter wheat previously grew, runways, hangers, and Quonset huts took their places. Sometimes would-be pilots overshot the runway taking off or coming in, tangling in some corn at the end of the runway; but only 11 casualties were reported at McCook from the pilot training. Day reported that he and his crew were the first to try night flying and landing. All went well, but they did have to remove cornstalks from the landing gear.

During this time most of the people of America were engaged in the war. Some worked as volunteers for the Red Cross, packing bandages or parcels; others ran Red Cross canteens. Patriotic fervor filled the area with welcoming stations along the rails leading to the bases or at the points of departure overseas. Many of the small towns hosted fairs, festivals, and carnivals. McCook was a

Dot Day and Barbara Gaddy

stopping point for troop trains headed east and west. Each stop had the women of the town offering cookies and lemonade, letter-writing materials, and whatever else might show support for the young soldiers. Most of these women had someone serving or knew someone who was. The town of McCook was also proud of their air base and provided activities for the soldiers. One such activity was a carnival in the town.

It was at this carnival that the rangy young airman from Mississippi and Alabama met his intended. Although Eleanor Jane Johnston worked on the base as a switchboard operator, it was at the carnival the two met for the first time. Evidently, he fell fast for the pretty, petite daughter of a local dairy farmer. Eleanor had dark blonde hair, a warm smile, sparkling blue eyes, dimples, and an easy conversational style.

Love and courtship time was short because of the upcoming overseas assignment. His next stop would be Charleston, South Carolina. As he transferred, she began her long bus journey across the country to join him. Their marriage certificate shows that William T. Day of Jackson, Mississippi, and Eleanor J. Johnston of McCook, Nebraska, were united in marriage at Trinity Methodist Church in Charleston, South Carolina, on 13 November 1943. The rites of marriage were performed by the Rev. R. Wright Spencer. The witnesses were Dewey R. Church and Maxine M. Bellamy. After Bill left for Brazil, Eleanor traveled to Mississippi to meet and live with Bill's parents, Frankie and Tennison, and his sister Katherine.

His records include various items of interest. Bill received a smallpox vaccination in August 1943 and a typhoid vaccination in September. His date of departure for the European theater of operations was 23 December 1943, with an arrival 26 January 1944. Part of the squadron did their training in Tucson, Arizona, while his group got their basic training in flying at McCook. The two parts met together in Charleston, South Carolina. The men were required

Battles: Glimpses of Truth

to sign statements of responsibility for their planes. From there they flew to Brazil in South America. The group left on Christmas Day, 1943.

Some of the squadron's personnel were transferred to Morrison Field, Florida, and flew the southern route to North Africa. Although the group flew interdiction and support missions, it engaged primarily in long range strikes against oil refineries, aircraft and munitions factories, and industrial areas, harbors, and airfields.

"Flying from Italy, the group flew 243 missions on over 150 primary targets in Italy, Yugoslavia, Austria, Bulgaria, Hungary, Romania, France, Germany, Czechoslovakia, Greece, and Poland. During this time, 13,389.19 tons of bombs were dropped during 7,091 sorties of enemy marshaling yards, oil refineries, bridges, installations, airdromes, and rail lines." (https://en.wikipedia.org/wiki/454th_Bombardment_Group.)

The B 24's spacious fuselage on the aircraft earned the nickname "Flying Boxcar." The B-17 was said to be a flying machine with guns and bombs added on. But the B-24 was built based on its being a gunship and bomber. The fuselage was built around two central bomb bays that could hold up to 8,000 pounds of ordnance in each compartment. However, it was not often fully loaded as that load decreased range and altitude. The United States Army Air Corps had requested a bomber with longer range, higher speed, and greater ceiling than the B-17. The Consolidated B-24 Liberator did not meet all the specifications. Compared to other aircraft at the time, it was relatively difficult to fly and had poor low-speed performance. A joke at its expense was that "the B-24 won't hold enough ice to chill your drink." The Davis wing was more susceptible to ice formation, causing distortions of the aerofoil section and resulting in a loss of lift.

The Liberator carried a crew of up to 10 people. The pilot and copilot sat alongside each other in the cockpit. The navigator and bombardier (he could double as a nose gunner) sat in the nose. The radio/radar operator sat behind the pilots facing sideways, sometimes doubling as a waist gunner. In the tail, up to four crew could be located in the waist, operating waist guns, a retractable lower ball turret and a tail gun turret, matching the nose turret ("454th Bombardment Group." *Wikipedia* 02/December/2020).

The 454th bombardment group was activated 01 June 1943 as a United States Army Air Corps combat unit of the 15th Air Force at Davis-Monthan Field near Tucson, Arizona. Training began immediately for Day's squadron, and the ground crew was sent on 03 July to Army Air Corps school of applied tactics at Orlando AAB, Florida. On 15 July, planes were sent from Davis Monthan to join them in Florida for practical field training. However, Day was part of the aircrew for the bomber.

Bill Day's experience in leaving Brazil resulted in his developing a fatalistic point of view regarding life and death. Part of the squadron left to go on to Africa; he and the rest of the crew of their plane, *The Standby,* were scheduled to leave the next morning to join the earlier group. His pilot and commander determined there was enough time for them to make the evening run. They made the flight successfully. As they waited the next day for the rest of the planes, the men learned a German U-boat had been off the shore of Brazil, picking off some of the planes. That, and other incidents, caused Bill to say, "When it's your time, it's your time."

Then after reaching Africa, they went up to Cerignola, Italy, with Italy having recently been taken by allied forces. They would make their bombing runs flying from Italy up into Germany. Bill was part of twenty-two successful missions flying as a side gunner or waist gunner.

A successful mission concluded with the analysis of the photography of a cameraman as a bomber crew flew over its targeted areas. When the crew made its return home, photo lab technicians removed cameras from the planes and began developing the film right away.

Battles: Glimpses of Truth

Trucks took the aircrew to the briefing room to verify each man by name and position in the plane to ensure that everyone got credit for completing the mission. Personal equipment including parachutes, flying suits, Mae Wests, escape kits, and oxygen masks were returned. Bombardier and navigator folders also were turned in; then they received some sort of refreshments. The air crews first reported news about any convoys spotted or aircraft in distress that needed to be re-transmitted right way. They also communicated information about personnel injuries and plane damage. They further noted comments about the bombing attack: time of the attack, the altitude, enemy encounters, equipment malfunctions, friendly fighter support, and types and locations of flak encountered (Germans mounted mobile guns for flak on rail cars.). Finally, crews were released to go to the mess hall or to their barracks. Gunners had to document thoroughly all claims that they had shot down an enemy aircraft. They had to be able to say where the craft was hit, how much damage was done, and how the plane looked and flew. This information was needed to give appropriate credit to the gunner. They told of tactics used by the enemy pilot.

With the return of the planes, maintenance crew personnel moved to identify problems for each of the Liberators and start the repair work. If the problems were significant, the plane might not go on the next mission. As soon as possible after the planes touched down, the mechanics and armorers checked to see what problems the crew had with equipment. They checked to see if the guns were jamming, if the turret motors behaved properly, and so on. Regardless of the time of the return, they started immediately and worked through the night.

The ground crew did not work by the clock. Many felt the plane belonged to them, not to the crew flying it. The most forlorn ground crew was the one whose plane did not return. Sometimes if an air crew managed to limp home late, they might find their possessions had already been distributed among others. Bill Day lived

121

in a tent next to the mess hall cook. It was the cook who told Day years later when they met that he had gathered up his personal stuff to send to Day's folks following Day's plane crash.

The first little 88mm cannon was Germany's main heavy anti-aircraft flak gun during World War II. When an 88 mm projector exploded at altitude, it sent out jagged metal fragments that tore through nearby aircraft. It also left a characteristic black cloud hanging in the sky. When the formation of aircraft was near flak zones, airmen were instructed to throw chaff, or metal strips, out the window of the planes. The strips were used to mislead the German flak radar about the altitude of the formation. With an airspeed around 300 mph during the bombing run, the planes were subject to anti-aircraft flak for about 10 minutes. If the ammunition hit close to its target, the air crew could feel and hear the impact of small shrapnel fragments. Even closer hits might disable the plane.

Gunners used an air-cooled Browning .50 caliber machine gun firing 750-850 bullets per minute at a velocity of 2,900 feet per second. Gunners fired in short bursts so gun barrels wouldn't overheat. "Routes were scheduled to avoid major flak areas as much as possible and mislead enemy fighters about the intended target. Each route, then, included several course changes until the initial point (IP) was reached. The IP was usually an unmistakable landmark, both visually and on radar. At the IP, the lead plane alerted the formation to turn toward the target by signal flares or by opening its bomb bay doors. All other planes promptly opened their own bomb bays and made the turn while simultaneously aligning in trail" ((*B24NET.* 392nd Bomb Group. Annette Tison. "Anatomy of a Bombing Mission." 2017. Accessed 4 January 2024.)

If necessary to bail out, the crew was directed not to waste time looking for portable oxygen, but just bail out without pulling the ripcord. The crew member would pass out for a couple of minutes but would come to and have ample time to pull the ripcord and make a safe landing.

Battles: Glimpses of Truth

Above 20,000 feet altitude, the temperature inside the plane was usually -40 degrees. Without gloves, hands would freeze to the guns or metal. If the airman had to parachute from 20,000 feet, he was instructed to freefall so he didn't freeze to death when he opened his chute. His flight uniform consisted of heavy underwear, heavy socks, regular uniform shirt and pants, heavy electric jacket and electric pants (a sturdy suit with copper heating wire running throughout), electric gloves, heavy shoes that fit inside sheepskin boots, a wool scarf and, of course, a parachute. As one man recalled, they would often have a chest pack 'chute' as a back-up. "When aloft, add an oxygen mask, a flying helmet, goggles, and a flak jacket when needed. Finally (!), a steel GI helmet fitted on top of the flying helmet ... I never weighed all of these articles of clothing, but I would estimate the total to be at least 40 pounds before flak helmet and jacket – round it all off at 75+ pounds" (*B24NET*. 392nd Bomb Group. Annette Tison. "Anatomy of a Bombing Mission." 2017. Accessed 4 January 2024.).

Statistics published after the war by the Army Air Corps tell a dramatic story about the air war against Germany. During the war, 1,693,565 sorties were flown – a sortie defined as one aircraft airborne on a mission against the enemy. Of these missions, 89 percent were deemed effective. Mission accomplished! Flying these missions were 32,263 combat aircraft. Fifty-five percent of these planes were lost in action. On the other hand, 29,916 enemy aircraft were destroyed. On the human side, there were 94,565 American air combat casualties. Killed in action accounted for 30,099, with 13,660 wounded and evacuated. The remaining 51,106 were missing in action, POWs, evaders, and internees. Miracles of survival were numerous. Stalag Luft III held many fliers whose planes exploded in the air – disintegrated – yet one, two or more crew members survived. Some were blasted unconscious into the sky, and came to on the ground, their open parachutes beside them. Others were literally dug out of the wreckage of their crashed airplanes – horribly injured, yet survivors. ("The Story of Stalag Luft III." AFHI Virtual Museum. USAF Academy Special Collections Library and William Newmiller.)

There were countless instances of men surviving the catastrophic destruction of their aircraft high in the sky. The accounts of explosion and fire which left men unconscious in the air only to have them land safely by parachute were so common that in Stalag Luft III such survivors had difficulty finding an audience for the story. In the last year of the war the German leadership actually encouraged enraged civilians who had captured Allied airmen to wreak their vengeance on them for destroying their cities and killing their women and children. How many men died this way is known only to God. Fortunately, and to their credit, German military personnel aggressively defended shot-down airmen from such outrages.

Generally, waist gunners installed their guns, and ground crew personnel installed turret guns. The pilot(s) and crew chiefs walked around the plane for a final visual inspection. Parachute harnesses and Mae Wests were checked, chute packs and flak jackets placed at crew positions. Finally, the crew took their position for take-off – navigator, bombardier and nose gunner usually on the flight deck; engineer between the pilots; radio operator at his desk; and the other gunners in the waist area.

Ball turrets occupy a special place in aviation history. The B-24 and B-17 bombers are the only aircraft to have ball turrets. In the 392nd, their time in combat was limited to September 1943 through summer 1944. Due to its low ground clearance, a B-24's ball turret (BT) was housed in the fuselage just aft of the waist guns during takeoff and landing. Once lowered into position below the plane, the ball turret could move in a complete circle horizontally and rotate 90 degrees downward. Its gunner fired on enemy aircraft coming from any direction below.

Although the ball turret seems the most dangerous crew position, statistics show it was the safest. The Office of the Chief Surgeon, European Theater, analyzed the 8th Air Force battle casualties between June and August 1944. Of 1,117 casualties due to missiles, 20.9 percent were waist gunners, 17.6 percent were bombardiers, and 12.5 percent were tail gunners. Only 5.9 percent were ball turret gunners (*B24NET.* "392nd Bomb Group." Annette Tison. "Anatomy of a Bombing Mission." 2017. Accessed 4 January 2024.).

Of 963 casualties from flak, 21.6 percent were waist gunners, 15.8 percent were bombardiers, 13.2 percent were navigators, and 12.6 were tail gunners. Only 5.5 percent of flak casualties were ball turret gunners. Waist gunners stood in front of open windows for hours on end. Electrically heated flying suits were therefore plugged in and rheostats adjusted to the desired warmth. When they worked, the suits were wonderful. There were many problems, though, especially for waist gunners. 576th gunner Bud Guillot on the *Kamenitsa* crew says, "Waist gunners were always kneeling and then standing up again, depending on where enemy fighters were and how they had to position their gun. As a result, the wires behind their knees would short out; sometimes they would burn the skin or catch fire." The suits didn't always heat evenly, with feet too cold and hands too hot, for example. "The only protection the plane offered was the 1/8th inch aluminum skin," he said. "The only armor-plating was steel around the back and sides of the pilot and copilot. Everyone else had to depend on the flak vests and helmets" (*B24NET.* "392nd Bomb Group." Annette Tison. "Anatomy of a Bombing Mission." 2017. Accessed 4 January 2024.)

Bill Day became a prisoner of war held by the Germans. On 13 April 1944 they had made their second mission to Budapest; they had only recently started bombing there. The plane began to have mechanical troubles and had to drop out from formation. At the time they were only five miles from the Yugoslavian border,

Dot Day and Barbara Gaddy

and they hoped to get parts there to make it back to base. Being out of formation left them vulnerable. A German fighter appeared and began shooting. The radio operator, serving as a waist gunner, was shot down; Bill turned his best friend over to find half of his head was gone. The shot that killed him would have gotten Bill had he not bent down to reload his gun, a task that could be done in two seconds. The ball turret gunner's gun had malfunctioned, so he left the turret, and was then hit and killed. Day, a side gunner, was also hit.

The men had to start bailing out because the plane was on fire; he passed out after opening his chute but woke on the way down. The German fighter circled them the whole time coming down possibly to check their location but also to collapse the chutes. Hungarian civilians noted where he was landing and took him to a farmhouse. The cameraman and he landed close together and were captured. The civilians tried to help him; they did not mistreat him but offered him food and wine. He was burnt on his face, hands, legs, and most of his clothes.

A man came up; in his interview Bill stated he was unsure at the time whether he was German or Hungarian and motioned for him to raise his hands; he complied. He was supposed to have his .45 with him but did not. Some men chose to carry their weapons, and some did not. Bill took his with him, but perhaps lost it when he was pushed from the burning plane. Approximately 25 civilians came up with the cameraman. The plantation owner spoke the word for "telephone"; Day told the cameraman Wilson that the owner had called in the police and that they were captured.

Discussing this memory was possibly too painful. He tossed in an unusual remark that the Danube separates Buda from Pest and they are not that far apart.

After the capture, the Hungarians confiscated the rings and watches of the men. After two hours with civilians, the men were turned over to someone in uniform.

He was taken to the hospital by a pickup along with four others. The men had been taught that if they were captured, they were to try to escape. However, he was wounded and sent to the hospital and never tried to leave. As a hospital, the facility left much to be desired. A private first-class soldier of the Hungarian army did his surgery without anesthesia. Later, the nuns redressed his wounds. Eventually one of the sisters found gangrene in his wound. Bill was returned to the dispensary for further treatment.

According to an article in the *Journal of the American Medical Association*, "Gas gangrene is a dreaded complication of severe soft tissue injuries in military and civilian practice. Its pathogenesis and typical manifestations are well known, and rather standard forms of treatment have evolved during and since World War II. A high index of suspicion and careful patient observation along with early and vigorous treatment can often prevent a fatal outcome." (CANIPE TL, HUDSPETH AS. Gas Gangrene Septicemia: Report of an Unusual Case. *Arch Surg.* 1964;89(3):544–545. doi:10.1001/archsurg.1964.01320030134023.)

The Hungarian hospital made use of an interpreter that spoke seven languages; the interpreter told him they were going to cut. To Bill, "cut" meant amputation, and he told them he did not want it. The interpreter explained they had to cut open the wound to clean out the gangrene. He credited the Hungarian private and the nuns with saving his life and his leg.

There were seven American boys in the same room. Across the street from the hospital was a place for the internment of Jews. Farther up the street was a garrison of Hungarian soldiers. The English bombed the hospital one night. None of them was hurt, but it was the scariest time of the war for him. He had no control; when flying and shooting, he had tasks to do. This night they were helpless.

After his hospital stay, he was sent to a federal prison in Budapest and was placed in solitary confinement. The first 24 to

Dot Day and Barbara Gaddy

48 hours there was no bad treatment, but no food either. "They had none to give me." There was no interrogation until he got out of his solitary confinement three months later.

He noted that the prisoners were given a very thick, tough bread about twice the size of a bun. They received a coal scuttle of water daily. He never knew the name of the prison. The cell had a steel door with just a peephole. It had four locks on the outside; his cell was upstairs on the second level of a three-stories high prison. The prison had a walkway inside. The cell itself was a 6' x 8' space with a mat on the floor for sleeping. There was a square hole high on the wall, about 10" x 10" where he could see outside. The guards did not want them to see outside.

If there was bombing in the area, he could not hear the door being opened. There was only one time that he was hit. He was looking outside when a guard entered his cell. Day was unaware of the guard's presence until the guard struck him.

"I started toward him, and he had a gun pointed at my stomach. If I had taken one more step, he would've shot me." Bill gave no further explanation about being hit. "The guards did not want us to look out the window, to sing, or whistle." When he was asked about toileting facilities, he noted they had another coal scuttle for answering nature's call. Once daily each morning, the guards threw in a piece of bread and a coal scuttle of water. The first three or so days he had bedbugs. He killed them on the wall and soon had a polka-dotted cell.

Later it was lice dotting the walls.

New prisoners were kept in solitary confinement while under interrogation and then moved into a collecting camp. After a week or ten days, they were sent in groups to a permanent camp such as Stalag Luft III for officers or Stalag VIB for enlisted men. A nearby hospital employing captured doctors and medical corpsmen received and cared for wounded prisoners.

Battles: Glimpses of Truth

Dulag Luft, located near Frankfurt am Main, was the Luftwaffe Aircrew Interrogation Center to which all Allied airmen were delivered as soon as possible after their capture. There, each new prisoner, while still trying to recover from the recent trauma of his shoot-down and capture, was skillfully interrogated for military information of value to the Germans. The German interrogators claimed that they regularly obtained the names of unit commanders, information on new tactics and new weapons, and order of battle from naive or careless U.S. airmen, without resort to torture.

He scratched out the number of days on the wall with his fingernail. After 28 days a German officer wanted him downstairs. This officer spoke fluent English with an accent and sounded like a Southerner. The officer asked about the bomb group; he answered that he could only tell his name, rank, and serial number. He asked where he was flying from. He refused to tell him.

"I'll send you back to rot."

"Well, you'll just have to send me."

The officer sent him but called him back again in three days and he asked the same question, and he gave the same answers. The officer told him, "We know you are not a spy." Then the officer started telling him things that he found out, even to how many missions he had flown. (If you went to northern Germany, you were credited with two missions; if France or Italy you were credited with one mission.) He was credited with 22 missions. Day's commanding officer was a Lieutenant Colonel Aynesworth, who later became a full colonel. The German officer told him that he knew he had gone up to Italy. The 454th Bombardment Group was the first to go up into parts of Italy to make shorter bombing runs. The officer also listed the squad commanders and other groups and asked if this was right.

He told Day that his friend with a little more seniority was in Florida and that American newspapers gave them all the information. He knew the day of Day's departure from the states and also personal details about when and where he finished school.

He was in the federal prison for one month. He noted, "All you could do was just be there." The rest of his crew went somewhere else. He did not connect with any of them until a few years before his death when he attended group reunions. He discovered he and the bombardier were both sent to the hospital. The cameraman was a fill-in; it was his first time flying with their crew. He was the one who put the chute on the tail gunner and saved his life.

He was moved from the federal prison after that last interrogation. They were 24 in a room for a while. One guy came in late, asking questions, dressed like them. This guy was pulled out about 15 minutes before they left. He assumed he was a spy and decided not to trust anyone else. The men were loaded onto flatbed trucks and were trucked to the railroad yard. Civilians were very hostile along the route. It was July 1944; without the guards there to protect them, the men would have been harmed. The guards had to use machine guns pointed toward the civilians to keep them away.

It was about an hour before they were put into boxcars. The trip took about a week because tracks had to be repaired from the Allies' bombing raids; there was lots of delay. It was rumored the war was about over. Bill noted evidence to the contrary.

One day in an open area the Germans added boxcars to a flat car. They had equipment to lift the box painted with a red cross. Once they lifted it off, they rolled a new tank onto it. Then they lifted the box, placing it back over the car. There were also boxcars of 15-20 fighter planes. The war was not about over; these boxcars were transported under Red Cross ambulance emblems. The train wound its way through Vienna, Austria; from Austria to Berlin; from Berlin to Poland, across the Baltic Sea.

The train had no bathrooms. All used a hole in the boxcar. They had a wooden box with horse meat in it. Day ate some, saying it

Battles: Glimpses of Truth

was not bad. However, he was starved and had not had any meat and got dysentery.

One of the guards told him he had not been home in seven years. (Day understood some Hungarian but could not speak it.) They had one corporal and two privates as guards. The guard said more because Day responded. He and the other prisoners made room for the guard to stand by the window to see his home. The soldier had tears streaming down his cheeks as he saw his home as they passed by.

They were often reminded they were safer in the boxcars than out in the countryside and safer in the prison camps than out. The prisoners were on their way from Hungary to a prison camp in northern Poland.

The German system separated officers from enlisted men and sent them out to the various camps, which were known as Stalag Lufts. These airmen's camps were administered by the German Luftwaffe (Air Force) and the Abwehr (German military intelligence service). Once inside the wire, the new Kriegesgefangenen or "Kriegie," as the prisoners were called, was once more among his own.

In general, the camps were segmented by barbed wire into compounds, each of which contained several Lagers or barracks. These were segmented into rooms which held upwards of 40 men in triple-tier wooden bunks.

On July 21, 1944, the men were marched about two miles. It was not a forced march. The previous day had been a forced march with the German police dogs to make them run and bayonets to stick them if they lagged behind.

They were put into a loggia. There were two loggias or pens with 1,400 men in each loggia. He was put in building 4. The enlisted men and one Englishman were in one part: the officers, another. They had tents for overflow from the barracks.

Here they had American doctors to work on them. "Do you want to be repatriated?" Swiss and German doctors came to camp to verify he was unfit for further service. If deemed unfit, he could be exchanged for a German prisoner.

Bill Day was put on the exchange list at the end of December. He was to be repatriated on February 8, 1945. About a week later they started marching. Five hundred were going out through Switzerland.

From 3:00 p.m. to 9:00 a.m., they were locked up twenty to a room. They had to build their own bunks to have a place to sleep. The room had a stove but no fuel for the stove. If someone was missing at roll call, the rest of the group had to stand and wait until all were accounted for.

To eat, each had a bowl of sauerkraut. They also had loaves of brown bread. They weighed five pounds each and had to last a week. One boy picked up the loaves and accidentally dropped one on his toe. It was so heavy it broke his toe.

There was no socializing. It was too cold. They stayed inside. The short daylight hours contributed to there being nothing to do. He did not play baseball in prison that summer as some did. Some of the men had a secret radio with the BBC transmitting.

Two men shared a Red Cross parcel weekly – hardtack cookies, powdered milk, jelly, three packs of cigarettes, tuna, and some other items he did not remember. He stated the men probably would have starved without the Red Cross parcels. He noted the guards opened everything. He remembered eating a can of tuna that had been opened for two or three days before he got it. The Luftwaffe – German Air Force – were considered an elite group by the other German soldiers and were given special privileges. This translated to Air Corps prisoners being better treated than the infantrymen, who were sent out on work details. Some men with nothing to do went off their rockers. Day's philosophy became, "If I make it, I make it; if not, then not. There's nothing I can do about it."

Battles: Glimpses of Truth

The men were allowed to walk in groups of two if they were able. The loggia had fenced towers at each corner and in the middle. Inside a twenty-foot perimeter of the outside wire was a warning wire they were not to go over. He did not witness men going over the warning wire but heard of some who did and were shot. Supposedly it was intentional suicide.

They had padres offering religious services on Sunday. They were guarded, and he was unsure whether they were also captives. German fighter camps were near the loggia. Often as they returned from missions, the pilots buzzed the camp. Once a third plane in a group did not pull up in time and crashed in trees just beyond the camp. Some of the men cheered, but Day felt empathy; he realized that the pilots and crew were just like them. He did not see it as joyous. Another time a soldier had a metal pole, knocked into a live wire, and turned red. These two made sad memories for him.

He noted, "We had too much time to think; it affected our minds."

Other camps had work crews. Russian prisoners cleaned the Air Corps latrines because of the preferential status. Some people played cards. "There was no stealing – we felt for the other guy because all of us were in bad circumstances. We had to answer roll call twice a day, which was our only exercise. All the fellows were allowed to keep the Red Cross parcels, and we would have developed into walking scarecrows if we hadn't had them. Every month we were given two letterforms and two or three cards we could send home. During the whole 10 months I was a prisoner, I only received six to eight letters from home.

The interviewer asked if anyone had escaped or had tried to escape. "No, not from that camp. We knew it was safer to stay in camp and believed the war would soon be over. There had been past efforts, people digging tunnels, etc. Three guys in our camp had parts of a radio. They would meet, put the parts together, just a

Dot Day and Barbara Gaddy

short time, while the BBC was transmitting. We were able to keep up with what was happening."

He was also asked about memorable guards. "There was one guard – Big Stupe. He had been in the front lines and was sent back; he was mean. He would just as soon hit you with his rifle butt as to look at you." One account stated Big Stupe picked one man up by the hair of his head. Another said by his ears. Bill often wondered what happened to him, but he heard that the prisoners turned on him and killed him on the forced march after Day had left. (Note: One report accounted for this guard's death when the liberation took place. One member of the liberating forces asked the men if there had been guards who were especially cruel. The former prisoners pointed out Big Stupe. The soldier drew his pistol and shot him.) Day noted the guards were friendlier at the end because they knew what was going to happen.

One occasion two kids were clowning, and one jumped out of a shuttered window. A guard shot and killed him. They found out they had insane guards from the asylum. The double doors had a 2" x 6" strip to close it. One guard stepped from the barracks to the porch of the next one and was shot and killed. Another one of them was shot by his own men just clowning around.

During his time, he only talked to one other guy from Vicksburg, Mississippi. After the episode with the spy earlier, he did not trust anyone not to be a spy. In the camp a good bit of bartering was carried out – anteing up cigarettes to play poker, so many cigarettes for a can of Spam or jelly. Day noted prisoners were to be under the command of the commandant of the camp. He and the other prisoners learned pretty quickly it was best to do as they were told.

For repatriation they left camp as a group; about 500 of the prisoners were on a train and went down to Lake Constance into Switzerland. At the Swiss border the train stopped, and each man had to walk across the border bridge between Germany and

Battles: Glimpses of Truth

Switzerland. They swapped trains and went on down to Geneva, Switzerland, where they met the train of Germans for the exchange.

The train made its way to Paris, then Marseille. It was in Marseille, France, that he saw the American flag for the first time. It was overwhelming to the prisoners because they had been denied the opportunity to see it. He remembered, "The men were sincere in their emotions on seeing the flag."

In Marseille, they deloused and were issued new clothes. From there they boarded the Swedish luxury liner, the *Gripsholm*. They spent four days in the bay before setting out.

One of the attractions for the men was the places to eat. He noted, "You could order anything you wanted; it was just like a nightclub. I ordered a steak, but I could only eat two or three bites of it."

They came in at Long Island, and he saw the Statue of Liberty. Once dispersed, he was sent to the hospital in New York, New York. He spent two days in the hospital in New York and was then sent to a hospital in Jackson, Mississippi.

He was interviewed for an article in *The Clarion-Ledger* of Jackson as he was the first local soldier to be repatriated. The article included general comments about the former prisoners.

It told of 463 repatriates with dozens of "ill, wounded and maimed American soldiers, repatriated prisoners of war reached home yesterday in the exchange liner *Gripsholm*."

Headlines evidenced great cities lying in rubble with a visible drop in morale among German prison guards, despite still the arrogant behavior of Germany's Nazi-indoctrinated youth. Although these were subjects of discussion between the journalists and the repatriated POWs, the soldiers were unable to articulate how it felt to be in the U.S. One bombardier asked how it felt to see German cities in ruins, remarked, "It felt like a job well done."

Another soldier, a Jew, said he was told by an older German soldier of their regret at the treatment of the Jews. "You got the

Dot Day and Barbara Gaddy

opposite view from the young Nazis" ("Repatriates Release Facts inside Reich-Picture Germany Reeling by Blows." *The Clarion-Ledger* 23 Feb 1945, Friday, page 6.).

Day mentioned he started receiving treatment twelve years previous to his interview at the VA Hospital for his skin, nerves, heart, and frostbite.

When he entered the hospital in Jackson after his imprisonment, he had several burned areas on face, hands, and ears, plus a numb leg from shrapnel hitting his left calf, a heart murmur, and a paranoid hypervigilance.

"It's hard for someone who has not been through it to understand it. I am just glad not a lot have had to go through it. A lot of them had it much worse than I did. I was fortunate to be captured in the European theatre rather than the Pacific.

"I lost lots of buddies. If I had been in position six inches back one way or another, it would have been me shot, but it was my best friend. The experience makes you appreciate home, the United States of America. If those who don't appreciate would appreciate more of what they have ... we have not had combat in our front yards; it has been somewhere else. The American people need to appreciate that.

"When you are a prisoner of war, you are 'denied your rights;' dropped into a place where you know no one; you don't understand what your captors are saying to you. The worst part is being denied your rights."

Bill Day's military occupational specialty and number were flight maintenance gunner 748. He wore badges to signify he was a member of AAF Air Crew member (wings) and an AAF Tech Badge. He took part in the Rome-Arno Air-Offensive Europe. His earned decorations were the American Theater European-African-Middle Eastern with two bronze stars. He received a Good Conduct Air Medal with one bronze cluster. He earned a Purple Heart.

He departed Europe 8 February 1945 for the USA with arrival 21 February 1945. His continental service was one year, ten months and 2 days. His foreign service was one year, one month, and 28 days.

The report from the War Department noted operations during the period 1 April 1944 to 1 May 1944. "The squadron participated in 17 group missions, compiling a total of 130 sorties. Some of the important targets hit were Bucharest, Budapest, Bad Voslau, Sopia, Milan, Turin, Toulon, and Steyr."

The report stated Captain Corwin C. Grimes led in four missions. One important mission was to bomb Bucharest Marshalling Grounds: "Heavy, intense accurate flack (*sic*) was encountered. Photographs showed that good bombing was done. Hits were scored on the roundhouse, turntable, and many warehouses. Damage was also done to the [other] warehouses and buildings in the area. This bombing no doubt helped the Russian cause considerably since many supplies for the German army fighting on the eastern front passes through these yards."

A list of casualties for the mission to bomb Budapest Tokol Airdrome on 13 April 1944 includes the name of S/Sgt William T. Day. Three aircraft were lost, along with thirty-two crew members, two of whom were killed in action and another who died, possibly of wounds in captivity. Pilot and co-pilot were First Lieutenant Robert James Widmer and First Lieutenant John R. Smith. They were flying the Liberator from the base in Cerignola. They were identified as 738 (HE) Squadron, 454 Group, 304 Wing Base. Their target was the Evaluation Center.

An eyewitness report of Sgt. J.W. Gholson, a ball gunner in a different aircraft, tells of the crash: The first time we saw Lieutenant Smith in *Standby* he was about even with our right wing, apparently having cut across into our formation. He was losing altitude and cut to our left (behind us). One ME 210 made one pass at the plane (*Standby*) before returning with four others, which each made a pass at *Standby.* One fighter was shot down and crashed. Then *Standby* (2000 – 3000 feet below with one fighter on its tail) cut to our left at about a 20° glide, and the men started bailing out in pairs of two. I saw eight men bail out. From all indications the last two men were the pilot and copilot because the ship went completely out of control at that time. The ME 210 let one more burst into *Standby,* and it blew up."

Another War Department report contained the words of Clyde C. Campbell, 2nd Lieutenant, Air Corps bombardier: When we made a turn off the target and flew about five minutes, there were four ships below us out of formation. Ornsbee (in ship number 42–64485) was going down in a 30° glide when an ME 110 came in on him. With that glide established, the ME 110s peeled off. I saw 17 chutes come out of two planes, Lt. Smith's 42–52248 and Lieutenant Ornsbee's 42–54485. I saw both planes hit the ground and burst into flames. There was plenty of time in the glide for all men to get out.

Another photocopy of an 18 April 1944 document lists the names of two service members who were known to have used parachutes but whose status was unknown.

Day reported on one of these casualties: Sergeant John Warnke was in the ball turret and was shot in the back of the head after having crawled out of his turret. He left the turret because his guns jammed. He was sitting in an exposed position when hit; Day stated Warnke would have been safer in his ball turret. After having participated in ten missions, Warnke was believed to have been in the plane when it crashed somewhere in the vicinity of Szrgeo, Hungary.

First Lieutenant Robert E. Weber completed a casualty questionnaire and reported bailing out and that two men were left in the waist of the plane because they were believed to be dead – Sergeants Warnke and Parlett. He stated that Day was burned. Plus, Day was injured by bits of metal fragmentation.

Battles: Glimpses of Truth

Yet another document of 15 July 1949 shows a request for a status update of the following air crew members of aircraft B-24-H which crashed at Ziskoros, Hungary, 13 April 1944. In Day's crew all members were listed as honorably discharged, with two killed in action, and one dying the day after the crash. Day was discharged 31 October 1945.

A further update 21 June 1949 regarding incomplete information had a Pentagon liaison officer noting that there was no record of amputation on Day. On another casualty report on Sergeant Harry Parlett killed in action 13 April 1944, Day had written on the War Department individual casualty questionnaire that Parlett was firing close range at a fighter when he was hit in the face. The War Department noted he was reported as having half his face shot away. He participated in fifteen missions.

The crash occurred 13 April 1944.

The enlisted record report of separation listed William T. Day this morning an honorable discharge on 5 November 1945 at 11:45 AM. Paperwork was completed by Byron Kaysen, a captain in the Army Air Corps as personnel officer. Day's grade was technical sergeant in the Air Corps. He was married and had no dependents other than his wife. His address at the time of entry into the service was Satartia, Mississippi, in Yazoo County, Mississippi. He enlisted 31 October 1942 and was discharged three years later on 5 November 1945 in San Antonio, Texas.

During his investment he served one year 10 months and two days in the United States and one year one month and 28 days in foreign service. During his time in the United States service, he attended aerial gunnery school for six weeks and airplane mechanic school for 19 weeks. His mustering out pay was a total of $300 with $31.60 for travel pay. His permanent address at the time of mustering out was Route 2, Jackson, Mississippi. Like all servicemen, he served at the convenience of the government. His occupation was listed as flight maintenance gunner 748. His qualifying badges are an AAF Air Crew Member Badge (wings) and an AAF Tech Badge. He also was decorated with the American Theater European – African – Middle Eastern with two Bronze Stars. He also received a Good Conduct Air Medal with one Bronze Cluster. He earned a Purple Heart.

His discharge paper also shows that Day was a prisoner of war of Germany for nine months.

The Veterans Administration Regional Office in Jackson, Mississippi, did a summary of his service career. It noted at that time he was a 63-year-old WWII veteran with 40 percent service connected disability. "He participated in bombing missions over northern Italy, southern France, and Germany prior to 13 April 1944 when the veteran's B-24 was attacked and shot down over Hungary; he bailed out and was captured by enemy forces."

The VA summary detailed left leg flak wounds; back injuries; and facial, neck, back, and bilateral hand burns. Day was hospitalized in Budapest and underwent surgery on his left leg which had become gangrenous. He was incarcerated at POW facilities in Hungary and Poland (Stalag Luft III) before his repatriation.

Medical problems noted during his time of captivity were severe malnutrition, including a 60 pound weight loss; dysentery; diarrhea; and anxiety. He also detailed frozen feet and ears during his imprisonment.

After repatriation, Day returned stateside. He was hospitalized for a period at Foster General Hospital, Jackson, Mississippi, and continued in a convalescent leave home before his discharge from military service in October 1945. He had dental problems with several teeth pulled.

The VA reported on his civilian years. Mr. Day has lived in Jackson, Mississippi; Oakley, Mississippi; North Platte, Nebraska; and Crystal Springs, Mississippi, since his discharge from the military service. His primary employment was with Central Battery

Battles: Glimpses of Truth

Company, now Chloride, Incorporated, Jackson, Mississippi, from1956 to 1984 when he retired.

Bill Day passed away 10 April 1996 in Jefferson County, Birmingham, Alabama, in the VA hospital there. The VA hospital in Jackson, Mississippi, transferred him there for bypass surgery. The surgery was successful, but he had a post-operation myocardial infarction. He was buried in Jackson's Lakewood Cemetery near the gravesites of his parents.

PTSD? At the time of his seeking VA services, he mentioned occasional war-related nightmares. "It's only in the past five or six years that I have had problems." Day further related that his retirement and subsequently having more time on his hands might be contributing factors to his war-related nightmares and intrusive thoughts.

BLACK WATER
Gail Harvey-Walker

The hole in the boat starts off tiny and small
you hardly notice the water at all.
The blackness seeps in slowly at first;
then all of a sudden the dam will burst.
It swirls around your heart till you think you will die.
You can only drain the flood with the tears that you cry.
Have you felt the black waters cover your heart?
Sometimes from nowhere it seems to start.
Or maybe you know the cause of the pain
but you are helpless to stop the pouring rain?

May 20, 2006

INTROVERTED
EXCELLENCE
Barbara Gaddy

"It's Way Too Peopley Outside" – this is the inscription on a coffee mug I recently gave my middle child, Daniel Taylor. He and I share the characteristic of introversion. I understand his feelings completely!

In December of 1978, I was checked in at the hospital for the birth of my second child. However, the doctor told me, "The tests show that the baby's lungs are not fully developed yet. Go home and enjoy the holidays – come back after Christmas for your checkup and we'll see about a delivery date then." Right!! Never mind that this baby was already two weeks past his due date. So, I was checked out of the hospital and went home as I was advised. However, a couple of days later, on December 23, Daniel Joseph Taylor was born at almost 10 pounds and 23 ½ inches long. And his lungs were just fine! Maybe even then he was thinking, "It's Way Too Peopley Outside" – and just wanted to stay in his warm, peaceful surroundings of solitude.

Daniel and I truly enjoyed our Christmas together in the hospital. Two of the three wings of the hospital were closed for the holidays because people don't schedule elective surgeries at

Dot Day and Barbara Gaddy

Christmas time. It was quiet – Daniel was allowed to stay in my room with me much of the time – we bonded and snuggled – and slept. It was a wonderful time.

He was a happy baby, content to sit alone and play with his toys. I didn't realize at that time – or even during his childhood and teen years – that his introverted personality was most likely playing a huge part in his actions and reactions. As they say, *Hindsight is 20/20.*

This "big baby" grew into a "gentle giant" of a man – 6 feet 7 inches tall and I'm not sure of the weight – but he is a Big Man. Still very much introverted, enjoying alone time rather than group functions. But did I tell you that he is a red head? With blue eyes? Now, you know that being an introvert does not mean one is always quiet – they do speak out when something is important to them. But combine that with the typical red-head reaction and you have an interesting combination indeed. Daniel personified these characteristics completely – but when he did "go quiet" in situations, it was time for you to watch out!

In high school, Daniel played drums and cymbals. I'd always said that he "marched to his own drum beat" even before I came to realize fully his introverted personality. He "did his own thing" and was always good at whatever he decided he wanted to do.

Daniel and I also shared an interesting, difficult, and somewhat contentious relationship with my mother – his grandmother. Although I'm sure that she only wanted "the best" for me and for him, the way she went about trying to accomplish her desires didn't resonate with me as a pre-teen and teenager – that's the reason why I realized Daniel's reactions when he had similar experiences with his grandmother at those same ages. Her domineering perfectionism, as well as her stern belief that her opinion was the only "right" decision or belief, just pushed us away emotionally. It was difficult to say the least.

Battles: Glimpses of Truth

Daniel decided to grow his hair long – to donate to children with cancer. He told me that "some child with ginger hair will love getting hair that was his or her original color!!" Introverts have a quiet empathy that is sometimes overlooked. He is indeed a sensitive soul – and I love and appreciate that quality.

As my parents aged, I invited them to live with us – a decision I thought was the best for them. I hoped the relationship challenges would not be a negative factor. I was misguided in my hopes. I learned later – and from relatives with whom she had shared her reason for moving in with me – that she agreed to live with me in order "to straighten out my family." It seems she disagreed with the way I was rearing my children and was intent on changing their lives – and mine. And you know what they say about "Mama Bear" defending her cubs. All my life I had allowed her to dictate to me – at least in the public eye – but when my children became affected, I could not remain silent. On several occasions, I confronted my mother when she truly interfered with my discipline of or decisions for my children; and when she interfered with my daughter's plans for her wedding; or my older son's decision of a college major. But with Daniel, she was harmfully invasive.

Daniel was always respectful of me and of my parents; however, there came a time that he reached his limit and confronted his grandmother, too. Needless to say, tensions were ever-present with my mother.

During the two years my parents lived with me, my youngest child was accepted to the Mississippi School for Math and Science and left home as a high school sophomore. My oldest was at college. Daniel was graduating from high school and planned to live at home and pursue his education at a local community college. The increasing interference of his grandmother (as in going through the trash cans in his room to see if she could "find" any evidence of – of – I'm not really sure what she was trying to find) drove him away from home. (I understood because I left home for college the

Dot Day and Barbara Gaddy

day after I graduated from high school! I stayed conflicted between doing what I thought best for my parents and doing what I thought best for my children. An extremely difficult position that caused me much anxiety and depression.)

Daniel has a brilliant mind. His intelligence in math, science, analytical tactics, music, and much more amazes me. But this intelligence also led to Daniel's being bored in his college classes. But leaving home and enrolling in these classes afforded him the ability to be away from the incessant grandmother pressures he had been coping with at home.

He, like his mother years before, went a little "wild" that freshman year of college – yes, again I understood. He told me he just didn't feel right "wasting" my money for college tuition when he already knew everything that was being taught in the classes – and at that time he felt it was so ridiculous to sit through classes that were not teaching him anything. He left college after that year and moved to Baton Rouge, Louisiana. He did various things – creating sound responsive visuals for concerts, being a waiter at a restaurant – but he also got in with some more-than-wild friends. His experiences there were not positive for his lifestyle.

Meanwhile, back at my house. My mother had no grandchildren left at home to "correct" since they had all left for school or otherwise – and she decided that she and my father would return to her hometown. Daddy didn't want to leave, but my mother's domineering personality decided otherwise. Daddy cried – I cried – mother proceeded with her plan.

I tell you that to let you know that Daniel asked if he could come back and live at home while he "got on his feet." And there was no hesitation on my part for sure. I enjoyed having my son back at home. Playing in the local semi-pro hockey league was a highlight for him. He still struggled with the drug and alcohol influence of his Baton Rouge friends – and that struggle would continue for years in varying degrees. The pressures under which he had lived had taken their toll on him – trying to cope is not an easy task. I know – I understand.

Daniel was hired as a machining technician with a glass manufacturing company, where he worked for more than 18 years. While working there, another event that changed our lives forever occurred on August 29, 2005 – Hurricane Katrina. Our home was almost a mile inland from the Gulf Coast and fronted on a large bayou. At this time, my father had passed away, and my mother was living in an assisted living facility not far from my home. The facility had closed for the anticipated hurricane impact, and I had brought my mother to my home. As the hurricane got closer and stronger, my mother was increasingly more agitated. My brother lived closer to the area of predicted hurricane landfall and was evacuating. So, Daniel took my mother to meet him along the evacuation route to keep him from having to come south to my house and delay his evacuation in the already-bumper-to-bumper traffic. I tell you this to show Daniel's character – despite the contentious relationship, Daniel helped to get his grandmother to safety and evacuation with my brother.

When my mother died, Daniel once again demonstrated the depth of his character. He was somewhat of a "free spirit" and usually dressed the part in worn jeans and tees and by also allowing his gorgeous red/ginger hair to grow long. I knew he was going to drive back to the funeral in mother's hometown – but when I saw him, there had been a dramatic change. He appeared in a new suit and shoes, with a "traditional" men's haircut. When I commented, he just quietly said, "I did it out of respect for MayMay."

To shorten this story, I'll refer you to the companion story in this compilation – "SWIMMING KATRINA." We had guardian angels on our shoulders, arms, and legs that day as we swam for hours at the height of the waters and winds of the hurricane. My Daniel was a constant encourager and companion on that fateful day!

Dot Day and Barbara Gaddy

We lost three vehicles and a boat as a result of Hurricane Katrina – one of the vehicles was Daniel's. Dealing with insurance was a nightmare, and of course, we could not get claims settled immediately – and did not have enough money on hand to purchase him or us a vehicle. We were able to purchase him a bicycle, and he lived with his girlfriend at the time because she lived close enough to his place of work for him to commute via bike. That continued for a while because we had lost everything and had no place to live or transportation for ourselves. He never complained.

His employment time at this workplace was both good and bad for him. Good because it did provide income, especially when they remained operational following the devastation of Katrina when so many businesses in the area had been destroyed. Bad because as he continued to work there, he provided many services outside the scope of his "job description" to be of help to the company – computer programming their systems, running all the various machining mills and machines, providing quality assurance, creating quotes and bids for potential business jobs, and much more – the company requested and depended on him to do these things because of his skills, but because it "wasn't in his job description" for which he was hired originally, they would not increase his pay. Nor would they promote him. They liked being able to benefit from his skills without compensating him. It became a no-win situation for him, with no upward mobility or advancement opportunity. The small family-owned and run business was more interested in paying their family members than taking care of critical employees.

For a while, Daniel engaged in discussions with company management concerning his position and his pay. He tried calm conversation as well as more forceful discussion (Did I mention he is a red head?). After the second time one of the top family management persons told Daniel if he thought he could find something better, then do it, Daniel "went quiet." Management obviously didn't understand that introvert characteristic and thought that

Battles: Glimpses of Truth

Daniel was "ok" because of his quietness. But it was really completely opposite. Daniel had set his plan in motion.

Daniel interviewed at several local industries along the Gulf Coast where machining was a key skill. His challenge or obstacle was that for 18 years he had been machining glass components for military ships and submarines. The industries where he was interviewing needed someone with the skills to machine metal – a completely different skill set. Ingalls Shipbuilding told Daniel that they "wanted his mind and intelligence" and needed him to come work there, but he needed to get the specific training for machining metal. That provided Daniel another impetus as well as the information for what he needed to do for his future. This happened in the spring of the year.

The local community college (the one he had originally planned to attend when he graduated high school) was offering a master machinist course – three concentrated semesters beginning in the fall. He requested that his employer move him to second shift to allow him to enroll in the master machinist program. That would mean that he went to classes each day from 8 a.m.-2 p.m. and then worked from 2:30 p.m. until almost midnight. But he was willing to do that to increase his skill set and also to provide improved marketability in the industries. For months the management delayed a decision. Finally, Daniel told them, "I am going to school. I am going to do what I need to do to better myself. You cannot change my mind. Whether you move me to second shift or not, I will be enrolling in this course." The gentle giant had spoken. They understood his statement and moved him to second shift.

Fall came. The machining course began. Daniel started his more-than-year of attending classes for 6 hours each morning followed by 8-plus of work on second shift. Homework and assignments were completed in there somewhere! Weekends were for sleep and laundry! Oh, yes – because Daniel had been actively using a specific computer programming in his daily work, he was

Dot Day and Barbara Gaddy

able to assist the instructor in teaching that module of the course – helping her as well as the students who had no previous knowledge of it. He was given the option to "test out" of the computer programming portion of the course but decided instead to assist the instructor and help his classmates.

During the first semester of his studies, Daniel was contacted by Ingalls Shipbuilding. A meeting was scheduled with him to discuss his employment with them. Daniel was told, "When you interviewed with us in the spring, we knew we wanted you. But you didn't have the experience in machining metals. We've been watching to see what you did – and we see that you are in this master machinist course."

Daniel told them, "Well, you told me what I needed to do. So here I am doing it." Ingalls offered Daniel an immediate job with them, which he began in November of that same year – again working second shift to accommodate morning attendance in the machining course. Still a very challenging schedule. Ingalls' managers also told him that his previous employer absolutely did not realize what they had in Daniel – with his skill set and intelligence.

The foremen and managers at Ingalls knew Daniel's circumstances and worked with him as he began to use metal machining skills. As he completed the various training modules in the course, Ingalls moved Daniel to different machines to incorporate that knowledge into his work.

After over a year of very long days and weeks, Daniel completed the master machinist course. Not only that, he had enough credits from attending for that year after high school that he also received his Associate's Degree. And in addition to those accomplishments, he completed requirements for several National Machining Institute certificates.

The position at Ingalls has not been without its own challenges – learning different machines, learning different metals and parts for ships. He was moved from second shift to first shift to learn a

Battles: Glimpses of Truth

new machine. Then he was moved back to second shift to be able to complete parts that were begun on first shift and were needed on ship construction the next morning. His body struggled with "when is night-time for me to sleep?"

I'm not sure how he managed all this – determination, courage, intelligence, skill – and probably lots of coffee along the way.

Daniel is an inspiration to me. My red headed, introverted, gentle giant continues to "march to his own drum beat." He is my inspiration for introverted excellence and for overcoming obstacles.

And, we both still agree that "It's Way Too Peopley Outside."

IS GOD GOOD?

Patti Lamar

Edited by Barbara Gaddy

Ray Lamar was born to Raymond and Jerry Garland Lamar on Sept 25, 1950, on the Eastern Shore of Virginia, in the town Nassawadox, where Raymond worked as a produce broker seasonally. Ray followed in the footsteps of his father and grandfather, Ernest Garland, the founder of Crystal Produce Company, in 1923 – "the largest packing shed producer in the world" at that time.

Ray had a passion for all things related to nature, including selling potatoes straight out of the ground to buyers all up and down the eastern seaboard and even into Canada. He loved the fields where they grew, the feel of the dirt between his fingers. He loved hunting deer and ducks; he loved fishing at Lake Yucatan – his own special holy ground – also founded by Grandaddy Garland. His final adventure was finding downed trees and turning them into pieces of art – bowls and lamps – he loved watching the chips fly from the tips of his bowl gouges, watching the shape taking on a form that the wood spoke to him; the grain and colors which he saw first – God's gift to him!

He loved the Lord, he loved his family, and he loved his work! He was an animal lover; a dog-whisperer – he could train a dog to do anything he wanted him to – he loved to show off his dogs and

Dot Day and Barbara Gaddy

their tricks! And he especially loved it when friends would bring a new family pet and say, "Ray! I need some help teaching this boy some manners!" He'd have them minding their manners in no time!

Ray was not just a gentleman, but a gentle man. The women all loved him, and every man was his best bud. "Brothers" one of them said. "He was like my brother, like everybody's brother!"

As a dad, he was fun! He could be a little bit short-tempered, but he was always fair, and hated it if I grounded one of them … he would help them get around it if he could, without upsetting me too terribly bad.

As a husband he was perfectly imperfect. He was the best of me; I was the best of him. We met face to face on our first date, with our 5- and 10-year-old boys in tow. We went bowling, had pizza, and we knew before we knew, that lightning had struck. A week later we were engaged, and in six more weeks we were married … 31 years flew past like a flash, with children and grandchildren; retirement plans, life on the lake, and love as big as the sun.

We never saw this ending coming – we were cautious – we did all the stupid, dumb stuff, but we got Covid anyway – I got better, and he didn't, and the reasons for that is a whole other book. My Ray … my best friend, my love, my life … gone too soon, in a manner not worthy of a dog's death. But God took him, relieved him of his suffering, and left me here for a purpose which I intend to find and attack, full throttle! Ray will not have died in vain; he will be honored, and God's glory will be revealed as His plan is manifested through Ray's death! Whether in this world or beyond, we will know how God is using this great tragedy for His glory!

During Ray's hospitalization, I updated a year-old post, talking about how we say God is good when things are going our way. The note I wrote on the 6th midnight following Ray's being vented, and he was making "baby steps" progress toward coming off. At this time, I still didn't know that he'd been given RemD (Remdesivir)

Battles: Glimpses of Truth

against our written (on his arms) wishes, and so I was thankful for every tiny step forward, which got me thinking … random thoughts in my quiet time: You know how, when things are looking up in bad situations, we love to say God is so good? I think about that sometimes, and I consider the times when things aren't going so well, especially regarding the health of a loved one … does this mean that God isn't so good anymore? No, and I know we don't mean it like that; but as I sit here alone in this quiet moment and thank God for Ray's baby steps back to health, I'm so grateful, and He IS so good.

But then, what if we were sinking fast? Would I still honestly be able to say God is so good??? I might have to give it a few minutes, and stomp and cry and ask why, but yep – I could get there, because the Word says, "To be absent from the body is to be present with The Lord" – I mean, how much better could it get??? Eternity with Jesus. We sing, "And He walks with me and He talks with me," and so my goodness! He will walk and talk with us in person – and after ten thousand years, we'll just be getting warmed up! We'll have, "No less days to sing God's praise than when we first begun!" And, "Because He lives, we can face tomorrow," with a full heart and the confidence of a reunion more grand than anything we can begin to imagine. So yes, BECAUSE He loved us enough to go and prepare a place for us, I'd say, "God is good!" Wouldn't you? All the time! And all the time, God is good! (Ok!!! Well!!! I'm glad I got that worked out!)

I admit I'm happy with the good reports and scared of the bad ones; but today because of your prayers, we are strengthened, protected, provided for, and cared for beyond measure – and I just **know** something good is going to happen thru Ray's illness! And when it does, the Glory of God will be seen! "Did I not say if you believe you will see the glory of God?" Yes He did; I'm looking forward to it with great expectation! "GOD IS SO GOOD!!!" I love you all and covet those prayers!

And so nearly a year later, I sit alone in the quiet, listening to rain's steady beat upon the roof, with no chance of my sweet husband coming home to me; and I again contemplate this very important question … IS God good? As I said in the previous paragraphs, I did have to take a "few minutes" and stomp and cry and ask, "Why?" But the answer kept and keeps coming back to me … as that tube was being forced down my husband's throat, breaking my promise **never** to let that happen, a tiny whisper into my spirit shocked my cries into silence. "It's ok, Patti, something good is going to come from this!" I believed it then; I believe it now, and I pray every day for Him to lead my steps, to set my feet onto the path of whatever that "something good" is. Because the sacrifice of Ray's life was worth it to God in order to accomplish His will somewhere down the road, then it's worth it to me, too. I WANT to see how the glory of God will be revealed to us as believers, and more importantly, to unbelievers who may be saved because of all our testimonies.

He loved us enough to sacrifice His own son for us, even in our sin, offering us the free gift of salvation and life eternal in Glory, if we but believe. There is no greater love than that. Even in my brokenness and grief, through His Word, and through my new "c19/ffg family" (a Covid death advocacy group), He has provided comfort and peace and gives me strength and encouragement to make it through another day!

A year ago, I'd have never believed it! And so, MY answer to MY original question is, "Yes, MY God is Very, Very Good!!!"

NAKED ON THE BACK PORCH

Dot Day

"Sic' 'em, Harry!" Harry, the year-old blonde collie of my brother Sonny and me, and I both saw the gleaming green-yellow eyes as I opened the door of the smokehouse. Harry needed no further invitation to follow his instinct.

Mama wanted a jar of pickled peaches brought in for our ready-to-be-loaded Thanksgiving table. Daddy's recent heart attack meant that our pigs would go to the butcher, and the smokehouse had become a storage room for her canned goods. I was sent on my way, and Harry followed whoever was outside.

Harry obeyed before I finished my command. A horrible odor engulfed the smokehouse and us. What I thought was the neighbors' tabby was actually a wilder feline.

Our pup reacted faster than I did. He yelped in pain, and then rolled over and over, using his paws to swipe at his eyes. My eyes were also streaming tears from the toxic fumes. I couldn't lie down on the withered grass like Harry, but that might have been a better choice than what later followed.

As the skunk waddled off after expressing her queenly disdain for the disturbance, I focused my mind on the job at hand. I braved

Dot Day and Barbara Gaddy

the dark reaches of the old smokehouse without Harry's help. He had run for the pond, I guessed.

Proudly holding the pickled peaches, I scurried for the house and burst into the living room. Some of the relatives had arrived – Uncle Milton and Aunt Vondell, my older brother Joe and his wife Betty. Granny Pace, Aunt Vondell's mother, had come with them, and we were expecting more.

"Mama, I think I've been sprayed by a polecat!"

Joe laughed. He had already been turned down for a position in a Yazoo chemical plant when the company discovered he had no sense of smell. Like most of us fair-haired ones in the family, his face reddened as he chuckled.

The others grabbed their noses or handkerchiefs and muttered commands for me to get out.

I offered the jar of peaches to Mama and waited for her commands. *Was I supposed to stay outside? How long would it take for the smell to wear off?*

Mama became a Boot Camp drill instructor. "Gene, find Dot some clean clothes. Dot, get outside and wait on the back porch. Sonny, get the wash tub and fill it full of water. Betty, please heat some water so she won't freeze to death. Dot, outside, now!"

She meant business, and I headed out onto the back porch. Fortunately, this tenant house had a section of the back porch enclosed by three walls. The old farmhouse was a dogtrot with an enclosed hallway, its ends serving as entrances and exits. One end opened onto the back porch. On one side of that section was a bedroom, and the other was the dining room. Although it was somewhat protected, the back porch end faced north.

Sonny drew water from the deep water well on the back porch and filled the large washtub. Afterward, he left to find Harry. Georgene came out fussing. She was fully fourteen and a lot lazy. Her idea of washing dishes was to leave hard-to-wash items soaking in the sink or tucked away in the oven. Then she made herself

Battles: Glimpses of Truth

scarce. I knew enough not to relish being bathed and shampooed by Georgene.

A friend and future sister-in-law had lent her some trashy romance magazines. She was in a hurry and had no time to wait for water to boil and no compassion for a stinking and freezing younger sister. An eight-year-old sister was already a pest to a self-important teenager.

"Get in the tub. I have to wash your hair." She hoisted a large box of Tide detergent, no wasting of soap or shampoo to override the stench.

I balked. Ice-cold water lacked any appeal. "Wait for the hot water to warm it up," I begged.

She insisted.

I resisted.

My olfactory senses had long ago vanished, and I was more concerned with my chattering teeth and extra-large goose pimples than with her discomfort at the scent of a polecat. Six years older than I, Gene was more determined, or I had misestimated her strength. She grabbed me under my arms from behind and dropped me into the water.

The water overflowed, splashing her shoes. Her mood did not improve.

I howled and stood up. She threatened. "You can sit down and get it over with, or you can stand up and take an hour longer. Either way, you're getting clean."

Seeing some wisdom in her words, I sat again. The cold-water shampoo with detergent was the worst part; she had no desire to be careful around my eyes and proved it. But the cold rinse helped get the shampoo from my eyes and hair.

As we finished, I noticed my hands and feet were white, but the rest of me was a scrubbed red. Aunt Vondell came out with warm water. She added her insight; "Tomato juice will help take out some of that polecat odor." No one volunteered to go out to the smokehouse to get the tomato juice.

When I look back on the indignities of that day, I remember wanting as a child to feel special, to have something that was just about me or for me. As the eighth child of a family of eight I was pretty much taken for granted. But that one day I received special attention.

How special is it to have someone bathe and shampoo me? How special is it to be able to feast alone in front of the kitchen fireplace? How special, indeed.

VAGABOND
Gail Shows Bouldin

When I was a small child of two-and-a-half, my father died in a tractor accident and Mama was left to raise us alone.

At the time it was just Gwen and I. Mama remarried, to a truck driver when I was five and Gwen three. We moved a lot, never staying anyplace long. I once counted thirteen different schools by the time I was in the 7th grade.

We finally ended up close to Mama's hometown in the little town of Collins, Mississippi, where I met a sweet friend named Vivian. Having moved so much and never having time to make or keep a friend, I was scared to let myself have a friend. She was sweet and loving, and I was, too, until Mama and my stepdad started fighting. I knew it wouldn't be long before we would be pulling up roots and moving again.

I started pulling away from Vivian and saying mean things so she wouldn't like me. She would just respond," I know you don't mean that." I couldn't bear to lose my first real friend, and I knew I would. I continued saying hateful things when she would talk to me. Finally, she gave up and left me alone. I felt bad and tried to make up, but it was too late. She would not be friends with me again.

She was nice, but not my friend. Soon after, we moved to Laurel, Mississippi, the place I had been born. I was twelve years old.

Over the years I thought of her many times and tried every way I could to locate her but was unable to. Finally, I Googled her name and even though she had a different last name, I recognized her immediately. Nearly fifty years had gone by. I sent her a private message but didn't get an answer. I tried to contact relatives with still no answer. Three years went by and one day I opened my Facebook and saw I had a message. She and her daughter were messing around to figure out her phone and found my message in another message folder.

She called me and I apologized for the way I had behaved all those years ago. She instantly said there was nothing to forgive. We became real friends although we never got a chance to meet again. We talked in some form several times a day for two years and planned to see each other. The first time something happened, and I couldn't meet her. She had been fighting cancer for several years but thought it was under control. A little over a year ago, it came back with a vengeance.

We talked even more about her faith and her concerns. I sent her little happies and cards to let her know I loved her. One was a cross necklace with a verse. She loved it and wore it everywhere. One evening she told me how sick she was; she couldn't eat. She said her sister was there to take care of her because her husband was so distraught.

The next day I tried to call and message her, but I got no answer. I connected with her sister finally who told me that Vivian had died early that morning. I cried all day, and a heavy sadness has been on my heart since, but I was blessed to know her. God gave me another chance to make things right. Sometimes you do get second chances.

By the time I was in the 7th grade I had been to 13 different schools as noted. As you can imagine, it was hard to make and keep

Battles: Glimpses of Truth

friends, so I was a loner. Finally, we settled in Magee, Mississippi, Mama's hometown, when I was fifteen. This was the third time of being back home. Mama had recently divorced and was having a hard time supporting herself and five girls on the small salary she made at the Universal Manufacturing Plant and side jobs at Zip's Cafe and the Frosty.

We were pretty much alone taking care of each other while Mama worked. I was the oldest, so I was left in charge of cooking. My sister just under me did the cleaning. To give you some idea of how I was, picture a tall, skinny, extremely shy girl with no self-confidence and no friends. We could not go anywhere, nor did we have money to spend. Then two things happened: I met another girl who also became my friend and a boy who later became my husband. It turns out my friendship lasted much longer than the marriage, but that's another story.

We girls would wait for Mama to go to work and then take off to the swimming pool or just walk around town. Paul Kennedy, the local police chief, would pick us up many times and take us home and threatened to tell Mama if we left the house again. I don't think he ever did because we surely would have had a fly swatter or house shoe on our back ends had he done so. We barely got by; some days right before payday we had biscuits and sugar syrup for breakfast and what Mama called "toodlum" gravy, which consisted of browned flour, grease, and water.

Evening meals would be something cheap like dried Lima beans, rice, and cornbread. There were times we ate better, but we never went hungry. Magee became our home for almost three years; a lifetime for us. My sister and I fell in love with brothers. They had their dad's car they shared, and we fought over whose night it was to get it. None of us had any money, so our dates were pretty simple. Later Mama married a truck driver who brought her a case of turkeys, and we all moved to Birmingham, Alabama.

Dot Day and Barbara Gaddy

We sisters disliked the stepfather, the turkeys, and Birmingham. We had left a place that had become home to our vagabond souls and started life once again in a strange place. Even now, 55 years later I still miss those years. The stepfather and Mama are long gone, and I'm an old lady; but when I get the chance to visit again, I am once more transported to a time and place where I will always be that young skinny girl who had finally found a home.

I HAVE MET THE ENEMY

Cindy Mount

Today, I was driving to the hospital to spend the day with my husband. Doug had been in the hospital for over a month now after he was involved in a motorcycle accident from losing control when he hit a patch of gravel on the road. I was listening to a CCEF podcast about self-pity. This is a subject of personal interest since God recently healed me of this distorted view of life. That is not to say I cannot still feel that way at times, but it no longer has a strong hold on me as it had for much of my life.

I glanced at my phone, perched on the magnetic mount in the car. A message from my friend, Dot Day, read, "Could you email me the prayer you posted today on Facebook so I can publish it in my next anthology, *Battles*? And write stories of your battles for it, too?" *What? You do not ask for much, do you, Dot?*

Earlier in the morning, I had posted Psalm 20:5 with a picture of King Jesus mounted on a white stallion. In the comments, I posted a prayer that I had written.

"Jesus, you are truly superb and awe-inspiring! Your promises of unfailing love always come to fruition. May your magnificence be apparent in our lives and your glory be evident in our world so we may witness your power and majesty. You alone are worthy of all blessings, honor, and glory!

"We trust you know what is best for us as we present our requests. We pray that You will answer and guide us in ways that surpass our understanding. As we abide in You, provide for our needs, even our desires. Fulfill Your purpose in every situation and request.

"We pray for peace in Jerusalem and Israel and ask for supernatural wisdom, discernment, and protection for their leaders and vulnerable people. You alone are Commander of Heaven's armies! All eyes are on You for what is needed. All glory, honor, and praise to You! Lord of Hosts!"

In response to Dot's request for a battle story, my initial thoughts went like this: All my life has felt like a battle. Frequently, we can believe we are the victim, and everyone is out to get us. But we do not always consider we can be enemies to ourselves. For many of my adult years, I have felt like that victim, and I wasted a lot of energy battling my circumstances, God, and my husband without realizing my biggest enemy was me.

"We are human, but we do not wage war as humans do. We use God's mighty weapons, not worldly weapons, to knock down the strongholds of human reasoning and to destroy false arguments. The truth is that, although, of course, we lead normal human lives, the battle we are fighting is on the spiritual level. Our battle is to bring down every deceptive fantasy and every imposing defense that men erect against the true knowledge of God. We even fight to capture every thought until it acknowledges the authority of Christ. Once we are sure of your obedience, we shall not shrink from dealing with those who refuse to obey."
2 Corinthians 10:3-4 NLT, Phillips

I did not know these verses as a young woman. My formative years were molded by my family life, circumstances, and the culture of the time I lived in. My interpretation of life and how to live it were grossly distorted, but I did not know. So, like everyone else, I did what I knew to do and hopefully learned from my mistakes. Except I kept making the same mistakes over and over. The definition of insanity is trying to do the same things repeatedly and expecting different results.

"Remember that the LORD your God led you on the entire journey these forty years in the wilderness so that He might humble you and test you to know what was in your heart; to prove your character, to uncover your motivations and find out whether you would obey His commands. He did it to teach you that people do not live by bread alone; rather, we live by every word that comes from the mouth of the LORD. He wanted you to understand that what makes you truly alive is not the bread you eat but following every word that comes from the mouth of the LORD." Deuteronomy 8:2-3 CSB, NLT, VOICE

As I read these scripture passages, I am reminded to "remember" what God has done in my life and family. Remember that the LORD your God led you on the entire journey. My whole life, He has been with me. How could I have ever felt alone? But I did. I did not know He was there. He led me through the wilderness of the unknown journey of life to humble me and prove my character, uncover the motivations of my heart, and find out whether I would obey His commands. How pitiful I have been in my unbelief and blindness. However, He did it to teach me that I cannot live by bread alone but by every word that comes from His mouth.

It is taking me a lifetime to get acquainted with Him. The journey has been challenging and even quite painful, not because of anything He did to me but because I did not know Him. I could not hear Him. Once I believed myself to be His child, I still did not

Dot Day and Barbara Gaddy

always hear or listen. By then, I had been conditioned to do things 'my way.' Yes, we live in a broken world. Adam and Eve started something when they listened to the wrong voice. But God has shown us through His word His every effort to tell us what we can do to receive His blessings.

"He remembered they were merely mortal, gone like a breath of wind that never returns." Psalm 78:39 NLT

He remembered! I am so grateful He did.

TO MY SON, ARCHIE RAY BUSH, JR., 1972-2009

Lynn Bush King

I love you, Archie. I miss you, son. We were so young when we just met you. I was eighteen and Ray, your dad, only twenty-one. You came three weeks early, weighing nine pounds. You entered the world in a breech position on January 5, 1972, at Hardy Wilson Memorial Hospital in Hazlehurst, Mississippi. Dr. L. D. Turner, a general practitioner, was our doctor.

Ray thought babies came the same size as puppies and couldn't believe your size. You slept in a bassinet by our beds. If you made the tiniest sound, he was the one who jumped up to check on you.

You came into the world feet first, ready to walk and explore. You started walking when you were nine months old with your feet turning out. Special high-top shoes helped correct that. You liked to be clean and neat from an early age. More than once, you took your diapers off and pottied in the corner of your playpen.

Sixteen months after your birth, your sister was born. You and she were close – playmates, companions, and confidants. Many

Dot Day and Barbara Gaddy

people thought the two of you were twins because you and she were so much alike.

Ray loved you so much, and you followed him everywhere. When we lived in Waynesboro, Mississippi, around 1974, you followed him to the garden. Ray didn't know how close you were, and his hoe punched you in the face. He picked you up and ran to the house. I couldn't tell who was hurt, both of you upset and covered in blood.

I love you, son. I think about you all the time.

When you were young, if anything had happened, you ran to me: "Mama's Fix-It Station," y'all said.

I miss my little boy so much. But I couldn't fix things – this time that mattered.

Last night I used my last two eggs for supper and set the empty carton on the counter for you. Then I burst out crying.

You also took care of me. Whether I needed a couple of eggs (you kept chickens in the back yard), or a ride to town, you were there for me. Chris and I were on our way to town and broke down near Johnson Road. A friend was going to take me home. As I was going to his truck, here you came!

I hollered at you, "I knew Baby Boy would rescue me!" When I totaled my van at three in the morning, you were the first one there. You stayed with me and then later towed the van home.

I miss you driving by and honking the horn or pulling up by the porch to see if I wanted to ride to WalMart.

I remember when you were five years old, and we almost lost you.

You and your dad accompanied a friend to the store in Cleveland, Mississippi. You stayed in the car while they went inside. Plundering, you found an unopened bottle of vodka, worked to get it open, and drank a good bit of it. Your dad rushed you to the hospital. Although you stopped breathing on the way, the doctors and nurses were able to save you. That time.

Battles: Glimpses of Truth

You loved hard. Not only Ray, but you also loved my dad very much. When Daddy died, you wouldn't set foot in Mama's house for several years.

You loved Nascar, football, and our family. You were just a big kid at heart. You loved children, and they loved you. You tried to act tough, but kids could tell you were "one of them!"

You deserved a good wife and a house full of kids. But the wrong kind of woman pegged you for a softie and took advantage of you until she tired and moved on.

When you were thirteen, we lived in Gautier, Mississippi. Every weekend you rode with your uncle to Crystal Springs. You started refusing to go to school and threatening to run away. The school advised me: I signed papers to have you put into the psychiatric unit at Singing River Hospital for three days.

Two policemen came over, chased you to your bedroom, and handcuffed you to take you to the hospital. I still hear the words, "I hate you, Mama! I hate you!"

The doctors told me you were just homesick for Crystal Springs, Mississippi. I started packing and brought all my children home.

It was years before I found out your uncle was letting you drink on those weekends, setting you on your way to becoming an alcoholic. I just didn't see it. I'm so sorry, Archie.

I was not the mom you deserved. All my children are beautiful, kind, loving, wonderful people. I'm so proud of them. They deserved so much better than a mother like me.

So many hard situations came into your life. In January 1996, you had returned from working in Louisiana, gone to the bank to cash your check, and were headed home. You stopped for a passing truck and then pulled out. A car came flying over the hill, and you hit the rear end of it. After you stopped and saw the other driver was okay, you left. We found out later that a truck came up the highway and hit the same car. The truck driver died instantly.

Dot Day and Barbara Gaddy

You went back to Louisiana for six months. When the grand jury indicted you for manslaughter, I went to pick you up. You turned yourself in.

In June the deceased man's brother stood up in court and screamed at you; the judge declared a mistrial. The trial was rescheduled for November, the Monday before Thanksgiving. You were found not guilty, but this was the beginning of your downfall.

So many of your friends let you down. J. beat you in the head with a trailer hitch ball. It took so many stitches to repair. T. didn't think breaking up with you was enough; she threw everything you had bought her into a tree in the middle of town. She thought it was funny, I suppose. She also aborted your first child.

L. took you to a party, where you were to be the guest of honor. Other 'friends' knocked you down, beat you and kicked you. You cried so long because you couldn't understand why a friend would do that.

B. lost your second child. After you and she married, she started cheating on you with her ex-boyfriend. You gave that one everything she ever asked for – nice house, cable television, swimming pool, and trips to Gulf Shores, Alabama; Talladega, Alabama; and New Orleans, Louisiana. She repaid your love by stomping your heart to death.

HAHAHA! I'm laughing so hard at what great friends you had! C. was dating your sister and helped himself to your wife.

Although you were somewhat involved in an accident in which a man died, you were found not guilty by a jury. A week later, I left your dad. I think you blamed yourself for our divorce. It had nothing to do with you, but now I don't think you realized that.

2002 – Frankie was in love with you. Jeremy was in love with Frankie. She became pregnant by you. On November 30, 2002, Jeremy shot and killed himself in your driveway. We (the family) all worried about you for a long time.

Battles: Glimpses of Truth

The first time you tried to kill yourself, you called it an accident. We believed you because of the timing. Your sister was due to come over that morning. She would have interrupted it. When I visited you on the psychiatric ward, we had a nice talk about changing your life, starting fresh. You even said, "I love you, Mama." For the first time. I never dreamed you were so calm and happy because you had decided you were going to try it again. On October 13, 2009, you turned off the air and turned on the gas.

The first night you were in the hospital, you stayed unconscious, but occasionally would open your eyes, look around, and say, "Where am I?" Before I could answer, you would be gone again.

Last night, I kept seeing you, in your casket, opening your eyes, and asking, "Where am I?" I wanted to run all the way to Pinola, Mississippi, and bring my baby boy home.

It's my fault. When you came out of the hospital, you were too okay. I should have gone down there every day, never left you alone. I should have made you take your medication and go to Region 8 [ed.-Mental Health Facility].

I failed you. I failed my whole family. I'm so tired of feeling. I don't want to feel anymore. This hurts too much.

I love you, Archie.

I LOVE YOU, ARCHIE!!!

This morning, I was asleep. I heard someone say, "He's here." I woke up listening for your truck, then started crying.

I can't do this anymore! I don't want to remember! I don't want to know! I don't want to feel anymore. I can't do this.

It hurts too much.

I go to sleep, seeing you lying dead in your bed, and I wake up with the picture still there.

Now, I have to tell your story. I can't remember the date. About a month ago, SHE had left you. SHE had been having an affair with a married man, A.'s wife called you and told you.

Dot Day and Barbara Gaddy

The next day, September 8, SHE called. SHE and her friend T. had gone to your house to get some of her things. They smelled gas and you were slurring your words and twitching. It took her over an hour to call anybody.

We rushed down there. We could smell the gas when we opened the door and could hear the machine running. You had pulled a large gas generator into your room, turned it on, and gone to sleep. I called an ambulance, then sat on the side of the bed, screaming at you and pounding your chest to keep you breathing. Someone put a fan in the room and opened all the doors to get the fumes out. You spent 5 days in the intensive care unit at Central Mississippi Medical Center.

Then, you were put in the psych ward for two days. You said it was a mistake; you didn't mean to do it. We believed you.

October 13 – T. pounded on my door at 9:00 a.m. SHE had called. You had texted her the night before about 11:00. Your text said you couldn't live without her. You were ending it. She waited until the next morning to call anyone. T. had been to the house and couldn't get in. I went down there. The gas fumes weren't so strong this time. The machine had run out of gas long before. You were lying so peacefully, gone. Twice she left you to die.

Well, she wins! You're gone!

ZEB, GUNNER, and KYE

Barbara Gaddy

The Mississippi River is a beautiful place. It calls to those who enjoy and revel in the outdoors – in the adventure – of the beauty of nature, and of the majesty of the river itself. The Mississippi River can reach a mile wide in places and can be more than 100 feet deep in spots. In some locations the currents of the river's water are unsuspectingly dangerous.

On December 3, 2020, the Mississippi River became the enemy for two young hunters – Gunner Palmer and Zeb Hughes.

Gunner, 16, of Hazlehurst, Mississippi and Zeb, 21, of Wesson, Mississippi, were scouting for ducks south of Vicksburg as they made plans for a hunt the next day. When the boys did not return that day, an intensive search was launched.

Many organizations and individuals joined in the search for the two: Cajun Navy volunteers; Mississippi Department of Wildlife, Fisheries and Parks personnel; Warren County and Madison Parish deputies; the U.S. Coast Guard; and 28 members of the Central Mississippi Overland Search and Rescue Team, composed of police and firefighters from around the state. Family and friends – and even strangers – from the community and nearby areas gathered on land and in the river. A private aircraft and another plane from Madison Parish in Louisiana participated in the search.

Dot Day and Barbara Gaddy

The truck and boat trailer the two were using were located at the Letourneau boat landing in Vicksburg, Mississippi. The following day the boat they were using was found capsized and damaged on Middle Ground Island in Port Gibson, Mississippi. Investigators also found their safety vests and hunting gear during the early days of the search. But that's where the search grew cold. Nothing else was ever found.

In November 2022, the low water levels of the Mississippi River made it possible for renewed search efforts. Boats were launched, cadaver dogs were employed – all to locate the two boys and their canine companion as well as others whose lives had been lost to the river.

At the end of the renewed search efforts, the results were disappointingly the same, with no additional evidence of the boys being found.

The emotional rollercoaster that these families and their friends have been on – and continue to endure – is documented in a collection of Facebook posts by family members, friends, and search participants. A few of these that share their deeply emotional and personal feelings and insights are shared here.

12/9/2020 post by Peyton

I'm missing you some kinda bad today, Gunner Palmer. You've been a little brother to me for a few years now. Zeb Hughes, I'm sorry we aren't as close as what we should be, Buddy. But lemme tell y'all, me and William C. (County) haven't quit looking for you boys. And I can promise y'all that we aren't gonna quit till we find y'all. I appreciate everyone who has helped look for these two goofy guys. Y'all please keep praying for these two and their families and friends.

12/18/2020 post by Gunner's friend Gannon

Battles: Glimpses of Truth

If you listen to the words God lays on Med Palmer's heart, not only will you learn more about the outdoors than you could ever imagine, but you will also find peace in what Our Lord has laid on Uncle Med to share to us. We haven't stopped praying, and we won't stop!

Love and miss you, Buddy!

12/19/2020 post by Johnathan

Spent today on the Mississippi River being Nick's "Spot Man." I'm super thankful for my friend and the opportunities we get to spend together.

As we closed out today, we gathered together and prayed. I heard something from a hurting father that has captured my heart.

Med Palmer, stated, "I want to be mad, but I can't. I love that river. If you get on it and don't see God, something is wrong."

The truth is you can see God all around you if you just look. His hand is on the small trickling stream and on the Mighty Mississippi. His hand is in the beauty of the sunrise and in the late summer thunder rumbles. His hand is on the tiny sparrow and the large gobbling Tom. If you would slow down just enough to look, you will see: He's got the whole world in His hand.

In the words of Mr. Med, "God's got me."

He sure does. I'm in His hand.

Morning post from Kim Palmer, Gunner's Mom

After a late morning start, forgetting to get gas in Crystal Springs and then realizing it's wayyyyy out in the country, I am on zero gas and having to stop at a sweet little old man's house and ask for help (by the way, 3rd time is the charm!). I finally made it to Port Gibson to meet Meghan and take lunch to our guys searching on the river. Then I went the wrong way and missed my turn twice. What a beginning to the day.

Dot Day and Barbara Gaddy

Just as we were able to get there, the guys had to come out anyway, as it was about to rain. So even though I was in a rush and getting frazzled and feeling like my day was going awry, I realized that everything happens in time. When it is supposed to. HIS time and not ours. This is a hard thing to accept for people that like to feel "in control" and on top of it all. So, take a breath and slow the rush and have faith that today will turn out the way it should be.

12/26/2020 Update by United Cajun Navy
Day 23 Update – Saturday evening
Today's search for the missing boys continued until dark with one helicopter, one airplane and CN (Cajun Navy) volunteer boats in a coordinated search.

Numerous officials were also involved in the search. United Cajun Navy Louisiana and United Cajun Navy Mississippi showed a couple live videos to volunteers in air and water coordination. The helicopter covered areas that boats couldn't get to as well as assisting with giving directions for boats to search.

The airplane covered much of the river in a visual search and assisted with relaying information to our Mobile Command team on the ground. We shared our information including search history to officials. Please continue to keep the families in your prayers and pray for the safety of the search teams.

1/1/2021 Update by Kim Palmer
Search resumes today for our boys, Gunner Palmer and Zeb Hughes. No news today. Who would have thought when we began this journey a month ago that we would see 2021 come before finding them? May this new year bring a miracle along with it. Asking for continuing prayers for all agencies and volunteers devoting their time and energies to help us. As always, we covet your prayers and support. Thank you.

Battles: Glimpses of Truth

1/1/2021 Update by United Cajun Navy

Day 29 Update – Friday

United Cajun Navy Louisiana and United Cajun Navy Mississippi have two boats on the Mississippi River today in the search for the missing boys.

We have had boats, volunteers on foot, drones, airplanes, and helicopters out searching for 26 of the past 29 days.

After taking all the past search history into account and speaking with the experts on the Mississippi River system design, we have continued to move our coordinated search efforts farther south. We will have planes in the air and more boats on the water once again Saturday and Sunday in our coordinated search efforts moving south.

We are still looking for volunteers with boats that have side scan or better sonar capable of navigating the Mississippi River.

Not everyone can assist in person, but EVERYONE can pray and share our posts. We are hoping once again to have a large-scale coordinated search effort this weekend. It's a New Year with many people volunteering, praying, and sharing our posts about the missing boys. We hope that everyone can continue to come TOGETHER to help.

It's not a contest, it's the right thing for us to do to help. NO one in our organization is getting paid, nor has United Cajun Navy asked for donations to help in the search. We are the UNITED CAJUN NAVY.

Update by United Cajun Navy Louisiana/United Cajun Navy Mississippi

Day 32 – Monday morning

Weather will be good today for search efforts with highs in mid-60s and mostly sunny. Two boats are on the water as well as one helicopter and one airplane in another coordinated search for the missing boys.

Numerous other boats are on the water as well.

Although weather conditions have been good for search efforts, water conditions are not as good.

The Mississippi River is rising, which means more debris floating down the river. Logs, trees, and all sorts of debris create navigation hazards. Also, barge traffic is extremely higher since January 1, creating more dangerous conditions. More than ever, prayers are needed for the families of the missing boys as well as safety and guidance of those involved in the search efforts.

Update by United Cajun Navy

Day 37 –Saturday evening

All five volunteer boats are on the water for the day in our United Cajun Navy Mississippi coordinated search for the missing boys.

The search went from Natchez, Mississippi, north for fifteen miles on both sides of the Mississippi River and after refueling in Vidalia, Louisiana, two of the five boats continued searching both sides for two miles south of Natchez, Mississippi.

The weather for tomorrow, Sunday, will be very cold with rain and possibly wintry mix forecast for tomorrow evening.

Low temperatures will be below freezing and forecast into the 20s the next few days with highs in upper 30s to lower 40s. Also, the Mississippi River is still rising, creating increasingly dangerous current and debris floating downstream. United Cajun Navy will closely monitor the weather conditions and make a decision whether to continue search efforts the next few days.

Please continue to pray for the families of the missing boys and the safety of volunteers involved in the search efforts.

Thanks for y'all's support.

Battles: Glimpses of Truth

1/24/2021 Update by Mercy Search & Rescue (NOTE: Mercy is the canine team member.)

This is just to show you what we are up against. This river literally has its own weather system of sorts. Mercy and I are off the river, as our team had to pull back. The fog got much thicker than this the farther we went; currents are terrible, and the barge traffic – on top of not being able to see – was causing the boat to come up out of the river and bottom out when we returned to the water. It was a bad situation, and as always … we have to ENSURE every bit of safety possible for our people. We all take risks each time we head out, but this was way beyond comfort.

The channel looks totally different … but once you cross into the Mississippi … everything changes.

With that said, we will still be out this week. The weather should start to clear, and we plan to use every second available. I am now stationed in Vicksburg, Mississippi, awaiting our team (other two organizations) to arrive. Huge thanks to Southeast Louisiana Underwater Search and Recovery 501c3 and Bruce's Legacy for making this operation possible. We are no good to families and authorities if we are not as safe as possible.

Day 49 post by Kim Palmer

When we are experiencing the deepest of pains and hurt, no one person can bring you out of those depths, quiet your fears, and slay the demons in your heart and mind. Everyone is in the same boat struggling to make it day to day sometimes; we all have hurt of some kind or another.

We all hurt; we just carry our burdens differently.

What pains us the most sometimes, is the knowledge that even though we are strong in our faith and love for God, we can't seem to understand why He feels the need to test us so often, so relentlessly. If we were running from Him, instead of towards Him with arms open wide, it would be easier to understand the constant trials we suffer through.

When I got off the phone with my aunt the other day, after talking about my uncle's heart issues, my friend looked at me and said, "Okay, we need to stop and have a conversation with God; tell him you need a break." To which I immediately laughed and agreed! Then later, my sister-in-law texted me, and in conversation she said, you have had your share of trials and tribulations. I agreed and said I appreciate the confidence He had, but dang ... Our Father knows each tear we will cry, each joy we will have in our lives, all pain we will endure, and He never lets go of us, even when we let go of Him.

"A broken heart ... I will not despise." Psalm 51:17. He will never allow you to drown in your tears; he promises to come and wipe away your tears and give you joy. "Weeping may endure for a night but joy cometh in the morning." Psalm 30:5

Well, we have had 49 nights of weeping, but some joys during the day. Thank God for family and friends, children, and grandchildren who can keep us going.

Our bottom line is faith, and faith is absolute ....

Update by Mercy Search & Rescue

Family is not only those that we are born into; it's also the people that God puts into our lives .... We are all meant to cross paths for one reason or another. He puts exactly whom we need where they should be.

What started off as a search for two young men has brought so many people into our lives. Mark and I were blessed to sit and meet with both families face to face this past week. We are forever bonded with new family, and we will continue to walk this journey beside them. Although at this time there is no recovery, Zeb and Gunner have sure left a legacy ... a legacy of many coming together, love, and blessings. These two young men are both the

Battles: Glimpses of Truth

epitome of everything that we wish our sons to become, and it has been an honor to serve and continue serving them and their families.

We now are faced with a moment of wait … waiting for the next step … a moment to absorb all that has been done and found. This has been a very difficult search from day one and continues to prove so. The family and we believe that whatever be God's will, it will be done. No one has given up. We will update as we can; but as you can imagine, information is very personal, and everyone is trying to process it all. We and the families appreciate all the prayers and well wishes.

Post by Med Palmer, Gunner's Dad

We weren't able to run the river today because of the weather conditions, so I decided to go sit in the deer stand. Gunner has had a particular deer that he has seen once bow hunting at 30 yards; he didn't have a good shot, so he let him walk. While sitting there this morning, thinking about how much I miss my hunting buddy, guess who walks out? There's no doubt I had an angel sitting with me.

1/29/2021 Update by United Cajun Navy Louisiana/United Cajun Navy Mississippi

UCN has made the difficult decision to discontinue our coordinated search efforts for the missing boys, Zeb and Gunner. This is the reason there have been no recent updates.

Although it is always our mission to help provide closure to families in these situations, that is not always the outcome. This search is one of the most resource intense and largest volunteer recovery efforts that UCN has ever assisted in, spanning over 30 days. Hundreds of volunteers stepped up and volunteered their time searching on foot as well as with resources such as airplanes, helicopters, drones, sonar, and boats. Volunteers faced the Mighty

Dot Day and Barbara Gaddy

Mississippi River challenges and ever-changing uncertainties that such a vast waterway and landscape bring.

Volunteers who are part of our UCN network are some of the most caring and selfless people that we've had the pleasure of working with; everything they did was without the benefit of financial assistance as men spent days away from their families. There were NO fundraisers done for United Cajun Navy Louisiana's or United Cajun Navy Mississippi's efforts in this search. We are neighbors helping neighbors because we can. We are proud to call all our volunteers a part of the United Cajun Navy family.

We also want to say thank you to the thousands of people around the world that followed and prayed daily for the boys, their families, and those involved in the search efforts. Special thanks to Lt. Gen. Russel Honore and the US Army Corps of Engineers for their input on the Mississippi River system design.

Although our organization is no longer involved, some are still involved, and we will continue to pray for the families of the missing boys as well as safety and guidance of those involved in the search efforts.

GREAT things happen when people work TOGETHER in a common goal.

1/31/2021 Update by Sharon Hughes, Zeb/s mother

Waiting is not usually easy on an average day, but this is the hardest waiting I've ever endured. Lord, get us through another day. I pray you block anything that stands in the way of recovering our boys, and please bless every person involved in the ongoing search and recovery effort. We trust you, Lord. Amen

2/1/2021

Good afternoon. Wanted to share with y'all a feel-good update by Kim Palmer

Ranger is Gunner's dog.

Battles: Glimpses of Truth

Duck hunting went a little different for Ranger this year. Bless his heart, we've been out for eight weeks on the boat and no ducks. He got excited about one last week, and we decided he needed to go.

Thank goodness for these friends of Gunners – they took Ranger with them this weekend!

We love you guys – Peyton, William, and Lauren.

2/2/2021 Update by Kim Palmer

Prayer requests for tomorrow please. Med Palmer will be back out tomorrow, searching for our boys, Gunner and Zeb.

Last week was tough; hearing that the group that came to help were unable to get any further than they did. Conditions are just much tougher here than was expected, but we appreciate the effort that was made.

We will continue to keep searching as the river and weather allow. Warren County Sheriff's Office and MDWFP will continue as well. Please know that we all continue to work together on this, as it is still an official investigation.

As hard as it is, we continue to trust that the Lord has a plan, and we will come to know it in His time. We continue to thank you for your support and prayers – they are invaluable.

2/9/2021 Update by Kim Palmer

We had a good run today, put in at Letourneau and made the run to Port Gibson and back. Water levels are up, and the morning was foggy. No changes.

Thank you for your continued prayers; there aren't words to express how much we appreciate the love and kindness shown us every day. Though it doesn't take away the pain, it helps make the days easier.

Dot Day and Barbara Gaddy

2/14/2021 – Sunday – Update via Sharon Hughes

Several months ago Zeb came home from my Mama and Daddy's house and said, "Mama!, I had no idea how much I favor Paw Paw! Look at these old photos I took pictures of!" As we looked at them, he said, "Paw Paw is the most consistent and dependable man I've ever known. He's the same everywhere he goes. That's how I want to be." Well, son, you were. And your legacy is proof of that.

2/21/2021 Update by Sharon Hughes

I'm trying, Lord. My mama heart just wants the answers.

3/3/2021 Update by Kim Palmer

Today marks three long months since our boys, Gunner Palmer and Zeb Hughes, went missing.

We met with Martin Pace, sheriff for Warren County, today at my office. Recovery efforts are still continuing, just scaling back to 2-3 days a week. MDWFP is continuing to do the same, and they will coordinate their efforts so that we will have someone on the river most days.

We are so thankful to the Warren County Sheriff's Office and the Mississippi Department of Wildlife Fisheries & Parks. Investigations are still ongoing with these departments.

Their hard work and support have been unfailing, and we are so grateful to them and each of you for your continuing prayers.

3/7/2021 Update by Kim Palmer

Searching continued today for Gunner Palmer and Zeb Hughes.

It was a pretty day and things went well. Members of Warren County Sheriff's Office and MDWFP were on the water as well as several boats from Copiah County. Thank you all for your help making today's run successful.

Battles: Glimpses of Truth

Thank you all for your prayers and love today and those that reached out to us. It was a rough day. Today was Gunner's 17th birthday and Zeb's is Tuesday the 9th.

As much as our hearts miss him, we know he's having a glorious day in heaven, and that gives us some peace and helps ease the pain.

Seventeen years ago this morning, we were headed to the hospital, and Med said come out on the back porch, and I did so even though we were late. He then yelped and some gobblers answered immediately – and he told Gunner to listen up. And there it all began, another turkey hunter.

This morning Med was watching the sunrise and heard some birds gobbling. God is good all the time. Though we may not understand the path we are on, we are holding firm in our faith and on the path.

3/9/2021 – Zeb's birthday – Update by Barry Hughes

Today was a bittersweet day. I miss my boy more than I can say, but I got to spend some time with him today on his birthday. The water was rough, and the wind was fierce early on; but as the day went on it turned into a beautiful day. I want so bad to be mad and hate that river, but as I look out across the river at the sunset all I can feel is peace and I know that's all Zeb feels, peace …

Happy birthday, baby boy. Daddy loves you.

Update by Sharon Hughes.

I've been on a roller coaster of emotions today, and I'm only halfway through. On this special day, I'd like to take a moment to ask everyone never to be fearful of mentioning Zeb's name to me. My biggest fear is that he will be forgotten. Please talk about him to me any time you'd like! He kept me laughing, and he continues making me laugh by the stories you share with me!! My heart needs your words.

Dot Day and Barbara Gaddy

3/10/2021 Update by Sharon Hughes

The most confusing part is simultaneously having a heart of gratitude while it is also completely shattered.

Update by Sharon Hughes

In the spring of 2020 Zeb informed me he was getting *another* black lab for duck hunting. I couldn't understand it … he already had Delta and had sent her to training. He really couldn't explain it, either. But God knew what was up. Kye went to training for about 4 months. He had only had him back about a month when the accident happened. God knew I would need Delta during this difficult time. She has been grieving just like we have. She checks Zeb's shop every time I let her out. She was so loyal to him and is now so loyal to me. Non-dog lovers won't understand it, but others will. She's my most beautiful and sweet girl.

4/16/2021 Update by Sharon Hughes

They say it's ok to "not be ok" sometimes. I've had a few of those days in a row. The capsized boat out from Port Fourchon has me almost paralyzed. I know what those families are feeling, and it's nearly unbearable. On top of that, I have a lot of anxiety when it comes to responding to people in a timely manner. So, you can only imagine the anxiety I am having when I just can't answer the phone or reply to a text for a few hours. I may be resting and trying to let my body recover from shutting down since the service; or I may just not be in an emotional state to answer or reply for a while. Additionally, I feel like I haven't thanked everyone quickly enough for being at Zeb's service in person or in spirit, for loving on us like you have in so many ways all these months, for the continued prayers, for the cards and gifts of pure love, for helping us search.

I just need to say this here in hopes that it may help me function a little better today, because I'll have at least attempted to make sure as many as possible know how grateful I am. Although I know

Battles: Glimpses of Truth

most people aren't expecting any type of thanks, there is something deep within me that causes me to thank and appreciate people profusely (sometimes to a degree of awkwardness! – I know, I'm sorry!!) Since December 3, I haven't been able to do that the way I once did ... and it burdens me constantly. I've never been on the receiving end of such generosity before.

Truth be told, there is no way to ever thank all of you appropriately. There will never be words to describe my gratitude. But it's there, pouring from my heart ... constantly. I need everyone to know that. I'm making my way toward working on more "thank you's." Hundreds have been sent (thanks to Marlee's helping me!). There are many more to go, some of those being to people very close to me – because your thank you card requires a lot more strength to write.

I'm just stuck right now – in lots of ways. You haven't been overlooked. Every day I hear of someone who was there with us searching and I had no idea. To those of you I never knew about, or may never know about ... I have thanked God for you, too. If you reach out and I'm not available, please know I am not avoiding you. I am just making it as best I can each day. I wish I had a better way to explain where I am at this moment, but I don't. I hope this helps you and me. And please, PLEASE, join me in prayer for the men on that capsized vessel, their families, the rescue workers, and authorities. Love in Christ – Sharon.

Update by Sharon Hughes, Zeb's mom

I am so grateful to Gunner's family and friends, Warren County Sheriff's Department, and MDWFP for their commitment to continue searching for Zeb and Gunner. I realize there are so many more than I'll ever know or could ever list.

Tonight I want to share my gratitude for the sacrifices made by E3 Environmental, LLC. (Clinton, Mississippi) and Mercy Search & Rescue (St. Amant, Louisiana) over the past 113 days. E3 has

Dot Day and Barbara Gaddy

provided a large river boat, captain and crew mate any time Mercy SAR is able to go on the river and search. We talked about it this week, and we think there are 29 or more days that they've provided a boat for Brandi Brignac to take one or more dogs out to search.

On Monday, after they searched, they graciously took us out on the water where the dogs have alerted many times over the course of this waiting. I was able to see for myself how Mercy alerts when she picks up on something and when she doesn't.

I could feel Zeb in the breeze and sense him all around me as I had an overwhelming peace and feeling of safety while I was out there. That, my friends, is a blessing straight from God. I have so many more words in my heart, but I can't quite seem to get them out like I'd like. I've taken a few days to process my experience and would now like to share with you here. "Thank you" will never be sufficient for the endless prayers, encouraging words, precious hugs, generous donations, and agape love that you've poured out on both boys' families during this time. Each of you is loved by me on a much deeper level than ever before in my life. Nothing is too small or under-appreciated! Everything matters. Thank you.

4/19/2021 Update by Zeb's dad

No matter where he is – give a boy a tailgate, a shot gun, and good dog, and he will feel right at home.

Other than God's love there's no greater love than what's painted in this picture. A lot of us have questioned how in the world Kye, Zeb's dog, didn't make it out. Making it out was never an option for Kye. His loyalty meant more to him than getting to shore. No matter what, he wasn't leaving Zeb's side. I can't say how grateful this old daddy is for that dog!!

Battles: Glimpses of Truth

4/20/2021 Update by Kim Palmer .

Out again on the water today, searching for our boys. The debris has lessened, and it seems water stages are lowering finally. The Warren County Sheriff's office was out as well. I want to share something with y'all. A week ago today they were searching for Kori Gauthier, the missing student from LSU. I received a call that a body had been found, but they hadn't identified it yet and that it may have been in the water for some time. For a moment my heart felt better than it has in some time, finally some relief for Zeb's family or ours.

That lasted about ten minutes until I found out that it was indeed a female and most likely the young woman. But for that ten minutes I felt renewed hope again, and even though it's taken me a week to get past it, it's getting better, day by day.

I share this for those with this same loss, for those that are longing to find their loved ones, for those families that are still looking out in the Gulf for their sons, husbands, brothers, or fathers. For those that have been looking for their loved ones for years.

God knows when we need our spirits lifted and our hope and hearts renewed. We still have faith that we will find our boys; and if not, we have comfort that they are with our Lord now and forever and we are grateful.

Please continue to pray for the families in the Gulf. The coming days will be even harder for them, but the whisper of a prayer will lift them up as we have been lifted by yours the last five months.

Editor's Note: At the time of this writing, Zeb, Gunner, and Kye – the faithful canine companion – have not been found. These families continue their endless rollercoaster – riding the many highs and lows of emotions, hopes, prayers, longing – and holding close the memories of Zeb, Gunner, and Kye.

My prayer for them as they continue their journey is echoed in the Bible passage Philippians 4:5-7:

Dot Day and Barbara Gaddy

"The Lord is near. Be anxious for nothing, but in everything by prayer and supplication with thanksgiving let your requests be made known to God. And the peace of God, which surpasses all comprehension, will guard your hearts and your minds in Christ Jesus."

NOTHING IN LIFE IS FREE

Janet Taylor-Perry

I was so ashamed of the way I grew up. For the longest time, I felt inferior to those around me.

First, I didn't know my father. I knew his name, but that was all. Many of my classmates said I was a bastard.

Second, having a mother who was old enough to be my grandmother made me cringe. Short, stout, black graying hair – she was nothing like my schoolmates' mothers, many of whom looked like fashion models.

Third, I wore hand-me-down clothes. My cousin Jeannie gave me her old things. One big problem with that was Jeannie was a hefty girl. I was almost anorexic-thin. Momma and Grandma did their best to make the clothes fit me. The few items that were store-bought came from Fred's or Bill's Dollar Stores.

Fourth, I lived in the Laurel Housing Projects. Very few of the people I went to school with knew of my circumstances. I would have been mortified for some of them to know – Jenny, Kathy, and Donna are the three I can name who knew about me *and* who came to my house.

Last on my whining list is that I received a welfare check every month, and I ate free lunch at school. I could not bear for some of the kids I went to junior high school with to know these things.

Dot Day and Barbara Gaddy

There had already been a few instances during sixth grade in which some of them had made fun of me.

A girl named Deborah had laughed at me and accused me of eavesdropping on her conversation with a girl named Martha. It was kind of hard not to hear them since one sat in front of me and the other sat beside me; they whispered throughout class on occasion. I wasn't eavesdropping when I overheard Deborah talking about "ironing" her very wavy hair. I asked her how she did that. All I could picture was her hair spread out on an ironing board and someone using a clothes iron to flatten her super-wavy hair. I had no clue there were ways of straightening hair. Mine at the time was straight as a board, and I used spongy pink rollers to give it some curl. Her snipe, "Let's talk later when Miss Big Ears isn't around," shocked me. I almost cried that she could be so mean. I never did anything to that girl. Martha was really very nice once Deborah, who was a preacher's kid, moved away.

A boy named Keith had made fun of me for not shaving my legs. My mother would not allow me to shave until I was thirteen. I told him so, and he and his friend Roger chortled. Yes, I had quite furry little spindly legs. But his words hurt so much that I went home and hid in the bathroom, locking the door. I took my mother's old double-edged razor, and not knowing I needed to at least wet my legs and use soap, I pulled the blade over my fur, which resulted in snagging a section of my shin and tearing a loooooong piece of skin from my body. I freaked out. I washed and washed and finally the bleeding stopped. I had to think fast of something to tell my mother when she saw my leg later. I told her I fell in PE.

Well, with these wounds on my heart, I wanted to shield myself from any other ridicule. The way I kept folks from knowing about the free lunch was sneaky. Every Monday, we had a homeroom meeting in which the teacher distributed our free lunch cards or anything else that needed to go home to parents, like report cards if it was that time. I always volunteered to pass out the lunch cards; thereby, keeping mine without anyone knowing.

I discovered that nothing in life is truly free. Especially, when one practices deception, even being willing to hurt others to hide the truth.

As Fate would have it, one morning, I forgot my lunch card.

We had no car when I was growing up; my mother couldn't drive anyway.

While we sat in our first period class, there was a knock at the classroom door. In came my mother. She had walked from home, in the cold, to bring me my lunch card so I wouldn't have to go hungry at lunchtime.

Oh, I was mortified when she held out that little green piece of cardboard. I just wanted to slide under my desk.

Years later, I heard many of the wealthier kids complaining because they couldn't get free lunch. *What*? Or I sometimes heard the kids moaning about their parents being mean to them. *What*?

A cruel reality dawned on me. I was lucky. I might have been poor, but I was loved.

How much of all our bellyaching was just teenage angst, I have no clue. But I did realize that unconditional love is free – and reciprocation is not required.

I can't imagine how much it must have hurt my mother when I dragged myself to meet her to take my lunch card from her and muttered, "How could you do this to me?" She never said a word about it. She just made sure I had it every morning from that day forward. Looking back, that is one action of mine that causes me to want to cry.

THE SWORDSMAN

Gail Harvey-Walker

WOUNDED hearts, like wounded birds,
Flop and flutter, but they just can't fly.
One who was meant to soar high above,
Has been grounded forever by cold, cruel words.

TONGUES, like swords, gleaming in the sun,
Stab at the heart, and slash at the soul.
When devastation is the swordsman's plan,
There will be no mercy; there's nowhere to run.

WORDS, like you're stupid, shut up, go away
Hurt so much worse when aimed at a child.
They seek out a home in the little one's heart
And won't be forgotten for a minute or a day.

HEARTS, easily broken, by a few simple letters
That are arranged in the ugly and horrible ways.
As quickly and quietly as a newborn baby's sigh
The swordsman's legacy will live on forever.

Dot Day and Barbara Gaddy

BLACK, like the night, their hearts must be,
To cause such pain in the innocent ones.
The anger and bitterness will go on and on
Unless the children can someday break free.

THE GROUND FORCES
Dot Day

Question: How many combat soldiers did it take to change a light bulb?

Answer: You'll never know; you had to be there.

Although this is a joke, truths are definitely hidden in it. Those who fought with the infantry saw loss and death and blood and guts and other images too graphic for us to imagine. They heard the sounds of anguish and pain; they heard their buddies cry out to have their pain ended. Sometimes the death toll was so high, reaching the point that they made no friends. One Vietnam veteran in his memoir tells of describing the flora and fauna of Vietnam in his letters home to his mother. He did so well she was unsure of his seeing actual combat.

He did.

I have known Scouts, Rangers, Delta Forces, paratroopers, privates, corporals, sergeants, medics, and embalmers. I know no particulars of the service they provided. The guidebook for departing the military does not say the following principle, but many adhere to it.

Compartmentalize those areas of pain and discomfort; don't be open to discuss those images that continue to

Dot Day and Barbara Gaddy

plague you. There are memories too disturbing to find words to fit. Don't startle at the fireworks or the first day of gun season in rural Mississippi. Whatever you do, don't let significant others know what you went through. Take the stance of vigilance wherever you are. It's not paranoia; you carry the knife and the gun for preparation. You are a trained killer, and there are enemies. Only another veteran of combat understands what you went through.

I don't have any stories from an infantryman, and that is not for a lack of trying. As a licensed marriage counselor, I worked with a couple of soldiers who served in support roles in combat zones. I offered my services pro bono to others. One man's response, "The only counselor I'll talk to is someone who has been in combat."

My wheelchair sometimes serves to knock down barriers; maybe I look innocent or trustworthy. I don't know; but, beware, I am a deceptive questioner with ulterior motives when I engage people in conversation. So, I have almost an interview.

My husband Charles and I were in line with our grocery buggy at Walmart. To my left, I noticed a young man with sandy colored hair moving products around the beverage refrigerator. He stuffed them inside his cargo pants and held a handful. He had on a uniform shirt for a company other than Walmart. I teased him about needing me to get a buggy or a basket for him. He said he had learned to pack tightly in Afghanistan.

I talked to him about my book project and asked if he was willing to be interviewed. Like all the others he said no. We continued talking. He told me he was deployed three times, two to Afghanistan and once to Iraq. He was a grunt – an on-the-ground soldier who was sent out on patrol with a small group. He showed me a place on his neck behind his right ear where he had been hit with shrapnel. "This is the wound that my mother found that let her know I had not been in Japan. I lied to her about my deployment."

Battles: Glimpses of Truth

Despite the wound and despite some hearing loss, the young man claimed to have no post traumatic symptoms. Questioned further, he admitted some bad dreams, some startling to loud noises, and avoidance of crowds. I encouraged his participation with other veterans at the VA hospital in Jackson. He said he had gone one time but the others there were Vietnam era.

Part of recovery involves helping others. A mantra almost of therapy is "the only way out is through." Even though he might think he doesn't need help, he can be the means to provide help to others.

He told me about having to pick up body parts of his friend that was running point on patrol. It was shrapnel from that mine on the path that wounded him. The medic dressed his wound, and he soldiered on.

Why do they do it – this fighting in foreign lands? They swear an oath to protect liberty. They help other countries throw down despotic regimes. Then they come home to a country filled with unwarranted violence. Do they hate this climate of fear and polarity, these attempts to build hatred among groups of people, this trade of security for our civil liberties, this practice of overspending that will lead to taxation that further progresses us to servitude, to become a country like those they helped?

We all compartmentalize. We deal with the urgent matters in our lives while maintaining our routines. We distract ourselves from reality. Meanwhile, all our soldiers, our troops, protect, defend, and serve. When the soldiers are deployed, their spouses and families also soldier on, doing the routine, facing the challenges, feeling the concern for their soldier.

I frequented a church with several veterans of overseas wars. One WWII veteran there never failed in his public prayers to pray passionately for those who serve. I sensed his memories gave his prayers special urgency.

Dot Day and Barbara Gaddy

Army, Air Force, Navy, Marine, Coast Guard, National Guard, Space Force, our defenders and patriots, our thank-you's are feeble, our prayers often hastily mumbled, but may you be kept strong in character, unswerving in service, seeking more to serve than to be served. May God protect you and bring you home.

Thank you for your service.

Postscript: My friend Janet and I are in the same writer's critique group. Here is her comment after reading this article:

This really hits home for me. I KNOW Rob has lied to me about what he did in the Army. He "catalogued" tapes in Germany. Okay – That does not explain his severe PTSD. He jumps out of his skin if I sneeze without warning. There are places where he "had moles removed." Okay – Once he let slip it was a scar from shrapnel, just like your guy in the essay. Hmmmmmm. I'm pretty sure cataloguing tapes didn't involve shrapnel. And anybody who has to sign a 99-year nondisclosure agreement isn't "cataloging" tapes. Supposedly those tapes have now been disclosed, as well as his "job description." Yep. That explains the redacted documents I saw. Ninety percent of the text was blacked out.

CUCUMBERS AND PICKLES
My Story of Battling PTSD
Josh Dawson

"What's the worst thing you've seen?" This is a common question asked of first responders by civilians. My usual response to this is "my paycheck" and end it with a chuckle. We know that these people don't mean to offend and simply are looking for some gruesome story riddled with gore. What people don't know is that this is one of the most damaging questions that can be asked of those of us who have experienced horror and tragedy on an intimate level. PTSD has become at the forefront of mental health conversation among veterans and first responders, rightfully so. This is a condition that has plagued us for decades.

I am one who suffers from PTSD as do many of my closest friends. We have united through pain and will allow each other to regale experiences and thoughts that we feel others would never understand. I have a problem talking to the uninitiated about the demons that live inside my mind day to day, hour to hour, minute by minute, second by second. As a person who has dedicated himself to caring for others, the most inconceivable action I could imagine is to bring harm to someone else.

Dot Day and Barbara Gaddy

I began to experience my symptoms many years ago when I was just becoming accustomed to being a paramedic. I was married at the time and a father. My story is not dissimilar to several others I have spoken to – in that the symptoms started slowly. These symptoms didn't even appear to be symptoms but simply my "having a bad day." I remember myself living the highs of helping someone feel better or stopping the deadly medical condition that has acutely sprung upon them. I also remember the frustrations and aggravations of running calls until the fatigue settled in and everything went grey. Then the calls would come in that would be total nonsense. It would be 3 a.m. when the radio would crackle "priority 1 to patient's residence for back pain" only to find that the patient had been suffering chronic back pain for 5 years, been seen at the ER the day before, and was out of pain pills again. My viewpoint of life began to skew towards a more cynical idea about society. I didn't feel as if this was anything strange at the time. Everyone I hung around felt the same way about society.

As the days continued and my outlook continued to follow this path, I became a husband who was short tempered; a father who was only present in form; and a son who was barely recognizable from that baby boy who was full of life and joy. My anger continued to swell, and I would lash out on my loved ones. I ended up being the very person I despised – the caregiver who hurt someone else. My home life suffered tremendously because of my attitude which, in turn, created even more stress. I began to stop feeling. My world went grey. There was no more joy or sorrow; there was only nothingness. This was the worst pain I had ever experienced. As all of this was spiraling downward, I lost someone very dear to me, my mother-in-law.

I had left work early one day because of being ill. My wife at the time and I went to see her mother and father the next day before taking me to retrieve my car from the station. We were only a few minutes from completing our hour drive when the phone rang. It

Battles: Glimpses of Truth

was her father on the other end in tears. "Your mama is lying on the floor not breathing" were his first words. The shock rushed over me like a black velvet cape. We immediately spun the car around and began racing to their home. The rescue call for 911 was activated while we raced to the house. The ambulance was about 30 minutes away from the scene, which meant that we would have to coach her father through CPR. Once the ambulance arrived, we changed our destination from their home to the closest hospital. We arrived at the familiar ER. I had worked there previously and knew all the crew in there. "They are bringing in a code, and it's my mother-in-law" was what I shouted as we entered through the doors.

I guided my wife to a conference room, and then I returned to the ER. The ambulance arrived, and there was my mother-in-law. The EMS crew was administering every medication they could to attempt to restart her heart, but nothing was happening. We all raced into Trauma 2 where she was transferred to the awaiting stretcher. The ER crew and I used every ounce of knowledge and equipment to try to reverse the inevitable. After 42 minutes I looked at the doctor and said, "That's it, time of death is …".

I left the area and went to the conference room where I discovered my wife and her father awaiting any word. I told them that we weren't able to revive her. I almost choked on those words as they fell out of my face.

I didn't realize at the time, but this was the beginning of the beginning. What lay ahead would be the most difficult challenge I have ever experienced. As my anxiety, depression, and disconnection worsened, my family life suffered. My behavior resulted in my losing my marriage. My children were too young to understand that Daddy was sick, and my parents were not well educated in mental health. I only realized later what kind of toll my mental health had on their health. I moved back in with my parents and threw myself into work. I would take every shift I could, so that I would be too busy to deal with my life. Suicidal thoughts ran

Dot Day and Barbara Gaddy

through my mind almost hourly. I didn't know at the time why I continued to struggle through this life instead of ending it. I began psychiatric healing through medication and weekly counseling. The worst was yet to come.

As my symptoms were increasing prior to my tipping point, insomnia was a way of life. At the peak of my symptoms, I would sleep less than 3 hours a week. I was unable to be in a crowd whatsoever. If I were to walk into a crowded store, I would immediately suffer severe chest pain, and I felt as if I were trying to breathe after being buried alive. I don't know what kind of provider I was, but my mind was not in the game. I felt alone. I felt disconnected from the world. I felt as if getting through today was insurmountable. My psychiatrist prescribed me a heavy dose of medications to try to help me sleep. As I began to sleep more, my feeling returned.

I had no understanding of what my mind was doing. I knew that the numbness was over, and the pain began. I cried almost every night for several hours while I would hide in an unoccupied area. I wanted to keep my feelings away from those that I loved. As I went through this, I would pray. I prayed for salvation, relief, anything that came to mind to help take me out of this place. This is the point when a friend told me one of the most prolific things I have heard, and something I live by today. As we were talking about the power of prayer, he told me, "Jesus has three answers to your prayers. Jesus either says 'yes,' 'no,' or 'not right now.'" I didn't fully understand what was meant by "not right now" at the time. As the healing continued, I felt as if I were living the line "one step forward, two steps back." It seemed that every time I would improve by any margin, something would happen that would knock me back. I continued to work on the ambulance and would share experiences with strangers every day.

As I lived my life with strangers, I had the opportunity to experience things that I didn't realize were possible. As I look back at some of these events, I see now that Jesus was continuously providing exactly what I needed. I would laugh at things patients would do. There would be situations where someone either took illicit drugs or not take their prescription and would have a psychotic break. Sometimes these events resulted in my seeing a naked person in public, doing whatever made sense to them. I have treated patients suffering from government brain scans to patients trying to hide from vampires. I have met Michael Jackson's wife on no less than 10 different occasions. I even had a person needing to meet Jesus, but not before we stopped by the strip club for one last hoorah. There would also be events that could not be explained: a grandmother who literally walked through fire to save her grandchildren from a burning home; a mother and daughter who collided head on with a drunk driver who were able to walk away from a vehicle that appeared to be scrap metal. I began to realize my purpose in life.

"We are put here to bear witness." This was the epiphany I had as time marched on, and the calls kept dropping. One thing that EMS is great at is having profound conversation in the most awkward places at the most inconvenient time. As my partner and I were traveling through what could only be called a hay field on our way to a person with respiratory distress, we were solving the problems of the world. We were extremely good at solving everyone else's problems. We weren't quite as good solving ours. As we arrived at the run-down shack of a home, we knew the patient and his family. We had been here plenty of times throughout our stay in this area. This patient was suffering stage IV lung cancer. The family did what they could to make life as comfortable as possible for this sweet patient. This night would be the last night we would have the privilege of talking to someone that could answer us back. As we watched our patient slowly slip into the Lord's embrace, we never left the bedside. Beep .. Beep ..... beep .... beep .... was marching from the speaker on our cardiac monitor. As the EKG rhythm went from weak into nothing, we

Dot Day and Barbara Gaddy

began to cry with the family. The brother was in the room. He was a reverend at the local church and began a prayer circle. He asked our Lord to welcome our patient into his arms and to thank him for taking away the pain and suffering our patient had for the past year. Upon completing the prayer, we all embraced individually. The patient's brother thanked my partner and me for being there. This was not uncommon when we experienced these kinds of events, but this time the statement struck me. Thinking back to the words being volleyed in the cab of the ambulance not 45 minutes prior to this, a thought occurred to me. Medics don't save lives. We don't always win when we fight the reaper. We don't always even help people. What we do is we witness. We are invited into a strange place full of strange people and we are asked to witness one of the most pivotal moments of these people's lives.

As I reflect on my purpose, I continue to think back to what my friend said. "Jesus gives us three answers." The third answer is now understood. "Not right now." As I bear witness to the most intimate moments of my patient's lives, I begin to realize that my trials and tribulations came with wisdom. Emotional wisdom is difficult to develop, and deep emotional wisdom is almost impossible to obtain unless you've lived through horrors. I have now come to believe that Jesus placed me in these places so that I can be someone who is capable of bearing witness with and to others. I have been privileged to provide a level of comfort for patients and families. If nothing else, I have helped someone.

I am now married to my best friend, and I have the honor of being a father to two wonderful children, as well as being a stepfather to two more who are incredible. I have lived, lost, loved, and healed.

My old partner made a statement that I would like to end with. He asked, "How do you make pickles?"

I answered, "Well – you take cucumbers and brine them in pickling salt."

Battles: Glimpses of Truth

He said, "Yes, but can you ever make a pickle return to being a cucumber?" As we know, you can never make a pickle become a cucumber again, and I can never be the same person I was before. I was a cucumber, pickled through overwhelming stress, and ultimately became a pickle.

A TALL GLASS OF TELL-IT-LIKE-IT-IS JUICE

David Ching

Rev. David Ching lived with the knowledge of his impending death from cancer for several years; however, in his physical struggle, he demonstrated grace and strength that provided encouragement and positivity for all who knew him. The below Facebook posts from David and those responding to him in his blog provide insight into his character and strength.

Thinking out loud: June 8, 2014

People say all the time, "Things have changed. It is a different world today." I agree that things have changed. We are more advanced. Technology is greater. Education is available to all who choose to partake in its knowledge. However, no matter the changes the world and its people have gone through while good or bad – one thing has not changed. The difference between right or wrong has never changed and never will. The conscience between our knowing right and wrong will never leave us either. Timothy tells us that by holding on to our faith and a good conscience that we keep ourselves from shipwrecking our faith and good character.

I Peter 3:16 tells us, *"Having a good conscience, so that, when you are slandered, those who revile your good behavior in Christ may be put to shame* (ESV).

Hebrews 10:22 goes on to say that since we have a high priest over the House of God, *"let us draw near with a sincere heart in full assurance of faith, having our hearts sprinkled clean from an evil conscience and our bodies washed with pure water"* (NIV).

Our conscience is like a little voice inside us that lets us know when something is right or wrong, even before we do it. Even though humankind is a selfish beast at times; our conscience after we have done something wrong convicts us of what we have done. That little voice also lets us know when what we are doing is right as well.

The problem is that we choose not to correct the wrong by asking for forgiveness because of our self-centered natures over-powering our thinking. One big problem we have is we have forgotten how to say, "No!" We see people daily falling into following the crowd even when they know what's going on or what is being done is wrong. I believe this is because we have gotten so far away from right that we have to follow something, and the crowd is what is in our face because we refuse to stand for the principles of right out of fear of not being politically correct or some other devalued reason. Our moral compass is broken, and we have dehumanized the beauty of life itself for ourselves and where others are concerned in the Christian and non-Christian realms of life.

Exodus 23:2 states, *"Do not follow the crowd in doing wrong. When you give testimony in a lawsuit, do not pervert justice by siding with the crowd"* (ESV).

Whether we believe in God or not, we know inside us what is right and what is wrong. Babies prove this to the world every day. I've seen babies take off their diapers and paint the walls with what was in them; and when caught, knew what they had done was wrong because they immediately tried to hide from their parents.

Battles: Glimpses of Truth

They never gave the child a "don't poo poo paint the walls class." I have seen babies who are held all the time start crying like something was hurting them; and as soon as they are picked up, they hush and start playing. They were never given a "get what you want by crying class." These are just examples I thought of off the top of my head. From birth, we all have that little voice inside us that tells us, "This is right, or this is wrong." What we seem to forget is there are consequences for the choices we make.

I hope your conscious is leading you in the right way; and if you are like me, I hope you have a God that will forgive you when your choices are wrong.

I Corinthians 4:4 states, *"My conscience is clear, but that does not make me innocent. It is the Lord who judges me"* (NIV).

August 10, 2014

Well, hello, world! I hope you all have had a better night than I had, and I hope your day is super as well. I can barely stand today; and when I do, all my muscles cramp up. Last night and yesterday were violently painful and disheartening to say the least. My mind is clouded, and I just feel very lethargic today; weak and just battered! I can barely eat and can only when I force feed myself. Yesterday's violent, painful, and blood-filled throwing up has me not wanting to eat anything or drink anything for that matter. Not a journey I would wish on anyone.

Everyone keeps saying don't claim your cancer. Well, if you don't claim it, then eventually it claims you. I have accepted the fact that from here on out is probably going to be violent and painfully harsh. But I am claiming it so I can still fight it with whatever strength I have left. This endless chemo and shots, I have come to the conclusion, are going to be bad; and if I don't claim it, my body is going to get claimed before the chemo stops working.

I have not felt this bad since the 13 days without food and water, rush emergency, no-sedative peg tube insertion and hospital

Dot Day and Barbara Gaddy

stay. Superman has had his tail handed to him the last few days. Welcome to the journey. Maybe it will help someone out there understand this cancer battle better, and so he may help his loved one tackle it better.

Anyway, have a great day and may the sun shine on your face and make you smile. I'm smiling – or maybe that's a grimace of pain – but the smile is in there somewhere. Just have to force it, or the pain will keep it hidden. Luv you guys!

Sent from Dorothy A. Day to David Ching: David, we love you and hate this for you. We humbly pray that God will be extra close and hold you in these very rough days. Lord, I don't know all of David's circumstances, but I imagine it is not his desire to see many others in these days. Lord, I pray for patient, loving, rested, kind care partners who realize when David is grimacing, he wants to smile. Lord, You promised never to leave us or forsake us. I pray this now for David; he knows you are near, but send him reminders in every thing he looks upon. He is, as we all are, so totally in Your hands. He has shown us his heart, and through showing his heart, has shown us Yours. Lord, we thank You so much for David's service and his intercessions for so many of us. You have blessed us so much through this faithful follower. Please bless him with an easing of the pain and discomfort. Lord, it is difficult to know the right words to pray, but we pray You will be merciful and gracious. Let David know how much he is loved by You and by so many Christians he has built up. We pray these blessings to a Holy and Loving Father Who gives good only.

August 14, 2014 – David Ching

Heavenly Father, thank You for allowing our joy to come this morning as the breath of life flows through us. It is because of this, Your love and grace, that we praise You first off today. You are the keeper of our hearts, and we ask that You allow our hearts to be

Battles: Glimpses of Truth

open and full of joy, mercy for others, and love for all things You created. Let us not take anything for granted today.

Father, humbly we ask that You take all those on our hearts today and touch them in a mighty way. Let them know You are with them, no matter what their situations may bring. Keep them close to You, and let each of us understand that Your grace builds everything we need to survive and push forward, no matter the battle we may face. It is through You, Lord, that we find courage and the strength we need.

Thank You, Lord, for another beautiful day and for answering our prayers according to Your will and purpose. Be with us as we go into the remainder of our day; keep us safe and let our freedom in You ring loud and true. In Jesus' name, Amen!

November 28, 2015

WOW! How excited, happy, overjoyed! I had to do everything within me not to let the tears flow. Angela, Billy, Alisha, David II, and Danielle, you guys got me good!

My bucket list of 5 things, which I cut down from 50 to the 5 that meant the most to me, was started today. All were to be able to travel except for two:

1. To live and continue to fight with my all to survive this cancer battle as God directs me to is still number one on my list.
2. To meet, spend time talking with, and if physically able to train with, my favorite UFC fighter, a brother in arms (Army Ranger and US Military Combative trainer) and all-around great friend (Social media). He is a man with a super character who loves his family: Colton Smith!

They all got me good when he walked up onto our porch headed in to visit me. What an awesome surprise, honor, and humbling

Dot Day and Barbara Gaddy

experience for me. When I saw him walking up the ramp I almost fell out of my chair. I was like, "Oh, crap, that's Colton who Angela is leading in here." I just truly am at a loss for words and finding it very hard to write about.

Angela, Alisha, and Colton did an awesome job at making this happen; and I pray Colton has a safe drive back to the airport and flight home to his wife and two boys. I thank them for sharing Colton with me. What a blessing it was to see his smiling face coming across our porch.

I have followed Colton for a long time through his UFC and MMA careers and his military career as well. He inspires me to keep fighting, no matter what. Many days I go find a video of his fights and place myself as him in the match beating the stuffing out of cancer. I'm sorry his opponents have to take a beating twice, but it helps me keep fighting, even if I might get a bruise or two and bleed a little. His character inspires the fighter in me to keep coming back for another round, no matter what cancer brings to the table.

I would like to thank Colton for asking if he could pray with Angela and me. What more could a person ask for in a hero – a man who loves God, his family, this country, and defends us on any call. He gives me a fighting spirit for life.

God gives me the strength to stand and fight. Colton's determination and will to give his all inspires me to keep fighting even when the odds and everything else are against me in doing my part.

Needless to say, "You guys got me good!" Angela said, "I am glad to see the light and smile in your eyes again and not just the smile on your face!"

Thank you all for making this broken-down vessel God is choosing to use, full of joy again with this visit. This put the icing on the cake.

Colton Smith, thank you for the gifts as well. I wondered why Angela Graham Ching washed my shirt. I had just worn it the other day and had it as my change-into morning shirt. My Colton fight shirt. Now everyone won't think I wear it all the time, even though I do ... lol. I have new Colton Smith shirts to wear; and the CD and signed fight night glove were awesome, too. Thank you. I love you guys!

They say, "We all die a little every day" and in a sense that is true, because none of us are growing younger. However, we never see the reality of that dying until we have some disease or have a doctor tell us, "You are terminal." BAM, our eyes become very open to the reality of death.

We all understand and see ourselves growing older each day and year that passes, but we never see that as we are dying – just aging. We just know that time passes, and we take how long for granted by thinking forever. The truth is that there is no forever in this lifetime where living is concerned. We are fascinated by vampires and other creatures that are immortal, because deep within us there is a desire to live forever, even if it doesn't show that reason to us until we are stricken with something like terminal cancer and draw nearer to death. The truth is, only our belief in God makes us immortal, because immortality is offered through God's Son Jesus. We don't know what that next life will truly bring, but we know only of what the Word of God promises. However, it is our only chance of immortality, and it does not cost us a dime, and we do not have to be bitten. No matter how many bats bite us, wolves or cats scratch us, or how much we want it to be one of those immortal creatures, Jesus is the Only Way to immortality.

Since being diagnosed, I have come face to face with the reality that I am dying, and it is truly a matter of time before that happens. The aging process has nothing whatsoever to do with it. The cancer is killing me, and I have accepted this reality that without some divine intervention, my days are limited. None of us knows when we are going to die; it is a possibility every day, but that reality isn't in our minds. We think we have all the time in the world. I

Dot Day and Barbara Gaddy

don't have that luxury because I know that I have something killing me. I see those with cancer being buried all the time; I see and feel the changes for the worse happening in me daily. I feel the pain growing stronger and deeper within me. I feel the breath getting shallower and shallower in each breath I take and every move I make. I know there is not one thing I can do that will change this eventual outcome for me. Therefore, I am blessed to know that I have immortality awaiting me once my days run out, because I am secure in what Jesus offered and I accepted.

Am I looking to rush this immortality? No, I am not! But I know that once it arrives, I will never have to feel pain or suffering; I will have a new body. The only fictional character that comes close would be a vampire, and it can still be killed. Once I have Jesus' offer of immortality in my heart, I will never die again.

As my journey began September 7, 2011, and the fight ensued, I have seen many with cancer come and go. I have seen those who had Jesus' promise, but I have seen many more that did not. I have spoken with some who accepted Jesus in our visits, and I watch their last days change for the better. However, I have spoken with many who did not accept Jesus, who shortened their lives and made more difficult last days for themselves with more pain, hurt and lost families, and a miserable lives in general. I have seen those without the promise become filled with so much hate toward God, family, and anyone who stayed around them that they died angry and alone. But, most of all, I have seen the fear in their eyes consume them totally until that final day. The promise of immortality through Jesus gives us hope, and the only thing stronger than fear is that hope. So, you can imagine what a life consumed by fear can do to a person. It consumes his mind, his heart, his soul, and eventually his body. It shortens life and kills any sense of finding happiness in his final days.

It saddens me to see this happening to people; there is so much more out there if they had the promise of Jesus in their hearts. It

Battles: Glimpses of Truth

is my prayer that whether a person has a terminal disease or not that he is building himself a heavenly home. One day this earthly place will no longer exist and an immortal home awaits those who do accept the promise. True happiness waits in this life and leads you peacefully into life immortal when that last day rolls in. You can accept it and enjoy what days are left without fear, or you can not accept it and suffer the added pain that overcoming, ruling, and consuming fear will bring in the final days of earthly existence – whether a disease, old age, or a car accident takes you. Acceptance is only a choice we each can make for ourselves. No one can do it for us.

Sent from Susan Jones Smith to David Ching, August 11, 2017:

Bro. David Ching, you've been on my mind. I was only friends with you on here, but I checked your posts every day. My cancer journey began on July 14, 2015. I was scared, unsure, wasn't sure of my future. But I was led by you to turn everything over to God. To be positive, and strong, even when I don't feel like it. My cancer came back March 2, 2017. I'm still following your lead, staying positive, and relying on my faith in God. I wanted you to know what an inspiration you were to me. I sent you a message and let you know the night before you passed away. I had no idea you'd be gone the next day. I was lost and felt alone. But I got myself together and was so glad for you! You had done it. You had got to meet God! What a blessing! And though everyone was grieving, I think they knew you were in Heaven, rejoicing in the reunion with family who had passed on.

Angela and your children, I know there is still a void in your lives. But know that your husband and father was a wonderful person, and his legacy lives on.

Editor's note: Susan also passed on with a legacy of a fight lost and won with cancer.

Dot Day and Barbara Gaddy

OBITUARY OF REV. DAVID CHING

Rev. David Ching, 50, of Crystal Springs, Mississippi, passed away December 23, 2015, at his residence.

He was born April 23, 1965, in Hazlehurst, Mississippi. He grew up in Crystal Springs and was a graduate of Union Academy. After serving ten years in the United States Army and United States Air Force, he served as pastor in the Nazarene Church. For the past twelve years he pastored churches in Granby, Missouri, and Houston, Mississippi. He also served as a member of the Houston, Mississippi, volunteer fire department. He graduated with a Bachelor's degree from Nazarene Bible College, Colorado Springs, Colorado, and went on to receive his Master of Divinity from Northwest Nazarene University, Nampa, Idaho.

FROM BOREDOM TO BRILLIANCE

Barbara Gaddy

Angela Carol is my "Angel Song" – my third child. She was born on a night when there was a magnificent meteor shower in the December sky, and the labor and delivery physicians gave me all sorts of grief about making them miss the spectacular show in the sky that night! But oh, what a special gift they delivered to me that night! I'm sure the doctors caught one of the stars in that shower and gave her to me.

As I said, Angela was my third; my first two were boys. So, I was already in for a different parenting adventure – or so I thought. She made it so easy. She fit right in with her brothers, playing in the pasture and creek with them (sometimes against the boys' wishes!). They rode go-carts, played with their toy trucks and cars in the pea gravel pile that my Daddy provided for them, making roadways and dumping gravel with their dump trucks.

She was an adventurous little girl and surely kept me on my toes. Several memorable experiences demonstrate her indomitable spirit.

One day, the boys were outside playing in the fenced backyard, and my precious little girl was playing in her room so quietly. I decided to sneak down the hallway and peek in on her to observe this angel at play. As I neared her room, the fragrance of Desitin – you know that thick, white, sticky ointment used for diaper rash? – wafted to my nostrils. And my steps picked up pace. When I arrived at the doorway to her room, she looked at me and smiled oh so sweetly, obviously proud of her Desitin painting on the windows, windowsills, and walls of her room. It took MUCH scrubbing with hot soapy water to remedy that situation.

When Angela was an older toddler, she gave this mom a heart-stopping encounter. I was standing at the wall-end of the counter in my child-proofed kitchen, talking on the telephone – not a cell phone because they had not been introduced – the kind of phone that was attached to the wall. Angela was playing quietly close by (are you seeing a theme here with Angela and "playing quietly"?) I turned around to see exactly where she was and what she was doing, only to find that she had moved a stool close to the cabinets on the opposite side of kitchen and climbed onto the counter! To let you know just how tall she was at this time, she could stand on tiptoe and reach the *top* shelf – the "safe place" for things like super glue. As she turned to look at me, I saw that one eye was completely shut – she had *super-glued* her eye shut!

She wasn't bothered or upset at all by this predicament. I am calm under pressure, but I can say that my heart did skip a few beats when I realized what she had done. That phone call was disconnected immediately, and I contacted our pediatrician to get his advice. His comments calmed my anxiety somewhat when he told me that she had not done any permanent damage to her eye, that super glue is actually used in eye surgeries. My curiosity was in overdrive wondering how this strong adhesive could not do harm to her eyesight. "How?" I asked. Super glue is used to plug puncture wounds in eyes to provide a base for the eye tissue as it grows back together. As the tissue reconnects, it pops the super glue plug

Battles: Glimpses of Truth

out. He recommended that I take her immediately to the ophthalmologist for additional evaluation and treatment.

I made that 35-mile trip to the ophthalmologist in record time! The treatment? If she was emotionally able to handle having her eye glued shut for at least a couple of weeks, the eyelid would separate on its own, albeit pulling her eyelashes out as it came unglued. Otherwise, the surgeon could cut her eyelids apart, but with a possibility of also cutting her eye. She was fine – never cried or became upset. For the next few weeks, her eyelids slowly separated starting at the inner corner of her eye. She looked a bit funny but never complained, her eyelashes grew back, and her eyesight received no damage.

A few weeks after the incident had resolved, I asked Angela why she was using the tube of super glue on her eye. Her response and reasoning were simple: "I was putting on eye makeup like Mommy."

Move forward a few years to tee-ball age. She and Daniel, her older brother by two years, were on the same tee-ball team one summer. Oh, they were so cute together in their uniforms of white shorts and orange team T-shirts. Time came for the first game, and Angela decided she did not want to play. Not wanting to force her, I encouraged her to wear her uniform and sit on the bench or the sideline and just be a cheerleader for the team. Not a good solution for her! She was convinced that I was trying to trick her into being in uniform and making her play when we got to the field. Her solution? When we got ready to leave for the game, she came out of her room wearing her Sunday dress, lace-topped socks, and white patent leather shoes.

Years later, when Angela was an adult, we were reminiscing about this, and I learned her side of the story. She had been hit in the back with a ball during tee-ball practice, and she did *not* want to go back out on that field. Wearing her Sunday dress to the game

Dot Day and Barbara Gaddy

was her insurance policy that neither the coach nor her mother would make her play. What a pretty cheerleader she was!

We moved to Ocean Springs, Mississippi, when Angela was in elementary school. She was active in elementary school and junior high activities, both academic and extracurricular. But during that time, I realized that one of the most detrimental threats to a student's education was developing: *boredom* in her classes. She was in the tenth grade and doing very well academically, being placed in advanced placement classes, sometimes with juniors and seniors. But she was battling boredom. I remember the day, early in the school year, that she came home frustrated and said, "The upperclassmen in my class ask such stupid questions!" She was really bored in the class – and teachers everywhere know that a bored student is extremely challenging as they try to teach to the varying levels of knowledge of the students in the class.

Her boredom continued, and then one day, she came home from school and announced, "I applied to go to the Mississippi School for Math and Science today." It seems that there had been a presentation of information to the tenth-grade students about the Mississippi School for Math and Science (MSMS) located in Columbus, Mississippi, on the campus of Mississippi University for Women. MSMS is a prestigious public high school specifically designed for academically gifted and talented students across the state. It provides a specialized and advanced educational experience – and I knew in my gut that my baby girl would be accepted, that I'd "lose her" from home two years earlier than I'd expected. She completed all the required essays and other application documents and went through the on-campus in-person interviews. And, as I predicted, she was accepted to complete her junior and senior high school years at that institution. She participated on the basketball team, swim team, and various clubs; but more importantly, she was challenged in her classes, no longer bored, and was provided the opportunities to excel and get above-and-beyond education that laid an excellent foundation for her college years.

Wanting to be as much a part of her upper-class high school experience as possible, I volunteered to be a senior class sponsor. I enjoyed meeting other parents and participating in the high school activities as we sponsored proms and senior class breakfasts and other fun events. I made many trips from the Mississippi Gulf Coast to Columbus during those two years! And I'm grateful to the guidance counselors at her high school who provided the information to these students, providing the opportunity to decide if MSMS was right for them, and encouraging them to apply if they were interested.

After graduating from MSMS Angela attended Mississippi State University (MSU) in Starkville, Mississippi. She majored in … English. That was a bit of a surprise to me after she'd attended the school for *math and science*, but I didn't question her choice for herself. She did well, and as a senior, she received the Payton Ward Williams Jr. Distinguished Writing Award for an essay she wrote analyzing James Joyce's *Ulysses*, which was published by the university.

I wasn't surprised when she told me she wanted to stay at MSU and pursue her master's degree. (Let's continue to keep that boredom in the distance!) What was a bit of a surprise, however, was that she enrolled for her master's in the field of *geology*! Once again, she did well, and served as a graduate assistant in the department of geology. She analyzed the mineral content of sand on Cat Island, off the coast of Mississippi. And for her thesis, she conducted research with support from the Mississippi Department of Transportation to analyze the Yazoo Clay formation in Mississippi.

How did that combination of degrees work out for her? Well, she has described her career path as a winding one. Immediately after college, she moved to Columbus, Ohio, and worked as a laboratory manager for a geotechnical testing firm. Then, she worked

Dot Day and Barbara Gaddy

for a major textbook publisher developing middle school earth science textbooks, later freelancing in the same field, and then as an editor for scientific journals. After taking a few years to raise her elementary-school aged kids (and during the pandemic), she now develops training materials for an engineering consulting firm and has started authoring her own book. Angela has always looked for engaging and challenging work – something that can hold her attention. She says yes to interesting opportunities and loves to learn along the way.

Angela also enjoys giving back and supporting the schools and activities her two kids are involved in. Starting in their preschool and continuing through elementary, middle, and now high schools, Angela has been an active member of parent-teacher organizations; led book fairs and fundraisers; chaperoned class field trips and band trips; and serves as a leader in her kids' scout troops.

Yes, my "Angel Song" is still lighting up the skies, blending the responsibilities of wife, mother, room mom, band mom, golf mom, theater mom, professional, Scoutmaster, the best little sister (just ask her brothers), marvelous daughter, and much more in a magical, kind, considerate, empowering, and life-enhancing way for all she meets and knows.

Angela made her own commitment as a young high school student to do something positive to quell the boredom. And she continues to turn boredom into brilliance with each step in her life.

DROUGHT

Dot Day

The hills turn brown, and the rain stays away.
Growth in my life stops and starts to decay;
Hope is in hiding, and of failure I am the prey.

Figures discussed, borrowing done,
fields cleared long before May –
Hope was in abundance, and life was so dear;
But the hills turn brown, and the rain stays away.

Planning and working, toiling past light of day,
My bequest is of earth and sweat and joy under the Son
But hope is in hiding; of failure I am the prey.

Little shoots of beans spring from the soil and become my pay.
One day at a time – all I must allow – no thought of the end.
The hills turn brown, and the rain stays away.

Two years – two years is all I can stay.
Two years of good crop would carry us through.
But hope is in hiding; of failure I am the prey.

Dot Day and Barbara Gaddy

Unless the rains come, I cannot be okay;
I'll leave my son insurance and legacy of toil
Because the hills turn brown, and the rain stays away.
Hope is in hiding; of failure I am the prey.

SWEET RELIEF
Pauline Rule

I live in the City of Jackson, Mississippi. I have lived in this location for twenty years. It is home. My dog knows just where to go when I open the door for him to go out. I feel safe and comfortable and grateful for my small house and the life I have built here. The interesting thing is that almost weekly friends and family who truly mean the best will ask me if I am ready to move out of the city to a safer place. I usually reply with, "When I feel unsafe, I will think about it." I am not sure if that is the honest answer or if I am just attempting to appease and appreciate their concern. Here is my story of how I responded to this question within me. There is not a right answer. It is only my answer. Who wants to live his life simply to arrive at the end safely? Like most choices, I am not as influenced by outside noise as much as the still small voice within me. Here is how I responded so far. This is my journey to safety.

I am not oblivious to the things that happen in my neighborhood. My family's thoughts are not without merit. The Dollar General across the street has been there for almost two years. Since it opened, a produce man was killed trying to mediate a family dispute, the door was broken in a night robbery, and the cash register was stolen in broad daylight. Less than a block away, a man was shot while driving and wrecked his car right across the street. The

Dot Day and Barbara Gaddy

convenience store I can see from my house has bullet holes in the windows. If that is not enough to make you think that I am weird, the city is famous for its horrible infrastructure. Our water crisis is so bad, not only did the state step in but the national government. The Mayor and City Council are always in a dispute about waste removal. You could fall into potholes and never be seen again. Even so, it is home.

I am unbelievably blessed. I am a minority in my neighborhood in many ways, but the most obvious is that I have had opportunities others have not had. I graduated with a degree in education. I have an amazing job in Integrity and Compliance at a Fortune 500 company. The pay is well above what I deserve, and the benefits are impressive. I have health insurance and get huge discounts on my internet and wireless phones. One benefit that I recently took advantage of was education reimbursement. I was at a career development meeting when I heard a speaker say she recently graduated with her master's degree in ethics. That appealed to me, given my current job assignment. I talked my boss and a co-worker into going back to school with me to work towards a Master's in Organizational Leadership/Ethics. This is where my journey to safety begins.

Claremont Lincoln University, Claremont, California, taught me so much about ethical behavior. It also taught me that I did not always respond ethically and that most of us think we are more ethical than we are. I learned all the theories and applicable practices. To receive your master's degree, you must complete a project. It can be a project of your own choosing, but it must have statistical merit and research. I started the project very broad wanting to tackle homelessness and crime in my neighborhood. Was there anything I could do that would not only change my neighborhood but would make it safer so that all the empty buildings became occupied, and the food desert could live again. As I researched, I saw the enormity of the social, mental, and logistical implications.

Battles: Glimpses of Truth

I was ashamed of how simplistically I had previously approached this subject. I saw how truly complex and overwhelming it could be. I learned that the high school dropout rate in my district is 52 percent. Forty-one percent of all the children here are born in poverty. The per capita income in my neighborhood was less than $30K a year vs the national average of $69K. The value of homes is $50K vs. the national average of $244K. The employment rate is 47 percent. Only 37 percent of the community have private health insurance. In the census, 654 people identified as homeless.

After months of studying how others are working to make an impact for their neighborhoods, I created a non-profit board of directors from the neighborhood. The board included a bus driver, two business owners, three co-workers, two pastors, and a high school principal. Our idea was to launch a non-profit bakery where we could provide food at a decent price and hire employees at a decent wage. We wanted high school juniors and seniors whom we could tutor to help them stay in school. It was clear that we were not looking to make drastic changes, just touch one life, open one building, and make a difference. We wanted to be part of the neighborhood. We named the future bakery "Sweet Relief." It was the treasurer's idea. Setting up the board satisfied my degree but not the longing in my soul to know my neighbors and become more a part of their lives and allow them to be part of mine. I yearned for an opportunity for each of us to find safety in the other.

Ethical studies introduced me to Father Greg Boyle. While I have never met the man, he has a profound influence on my life. His writings and his journey resonated with me. He is not oblivious to the world around him; he saw it all as an act of praise to the God who created all of us uniquely different and the same. His writings reminded me of some amazingly simple truths that I would weave into the fabric of my life. There are three that have been the cornerstones for me since the day I heard them. Number one is "You do not go to the margins to change people. You go to the margins so that you yourself will experience change." Number two, "You can return people to themselves by reminding them they are exactly what God intended when He created them." Number 3, "We ought to stand in awe of what people have to carry, rather than in judgement of how they carry it." If I can do these cornerstones justice, they may change your vision as much as they have mine. In my search for safety, these three simple truths guide me, they envelope me, and they teach me daily that I can do better and be better and live better than yesterday. They teach me my own shortcomings and my own insecurities. They allow me, "chief of sinners," to participate in restoration and grace. They remind me that I am exactly what God intended when He created me. That allows grace to wash away the stains of yesterday, so they do not impact tomorrow. The less baggage you carry the lighter the journey.

I can now write a book about how not to start a business. I will not bore you with the details, but the journey was not easy. It was the miracles along the way that kept us going. A board member came into some money just when we found the right building. He and his wife bought the building for the non-profit at an amazing price because of his negotiation skills. That was miracle number one. It was in the perfect spot in the neighborhood. The school who owned the land welcomed us with open arms. I searched Facebook Marketplace for the right equipment we would need, and I found a man selling the top-of-the-line shaved ice equipment. It just so happened that I bought it one hour before the next ten offers. That is what he told me when I went to pick it up. He did not just sell me the equipment; he took several hours with us that morning teaching us how to use it, telling us how to make our own ice, giving me a cash register, a menu from his store and showing me how the store operated and the must haves. He gave me recipes and an overall view of what it meant to run a shaved ice business. He would become one of the first teachers but not the last. This was miracle number two. There were applications, deposits, license, and food safety certifications to follow. There were utilities and supplies to buy. There was additional equipment to purchase. Cleaning, plumbing, and shelf building commenced. Six months later, on July 1, 2022, we were in business.

We were only open on weekends and two hours each evening. Many things happened to cause me to question my decision to start the business. There was a water crisis in the city, and we were down for a week because of the lack of water. Someone stole the copper cable, and the internet that ran my cash register was down for two weeks. The traffic was slow, and the people did not have money for nachos, cookies, and shaved ice. They could barely make necessities. I asked God if this was really what He wanted? I was seeking direction. That week I received a sign for the building from a co-worker with this message. "Sweet Relief Bakery – est. 2022." On the second line it read, "Ecclesiastes 9:7". It was so thoughtful but when I read the verse, it reminded me why I was there, and that God approved. Here is what the verse says, "Go eat your bread with joy, and drink your wine with a merry heart; For God has already approved your works." Prayers answered. Mission grounded. It was not about numbers or money or my plan. It was about people, relationships, and growth. It was a miracle that we made it to this point. My vision, joy and gladness were restored. The journey was just beginning. Miracle number three was so sweet.

I remember the day I met Kat. It would be almost eight months later that I knew his name. We quickly found a kindred spirit. He called me, "predyladie," which as you can tell is all one word. Kat was the most visible face in the neighborhood. He drives a white SUV and can be seen throughout the day going back and forth from one person to the other. He would come by every other day for nachos. Sometimes the SUV would be full of young men and other times his family. It made my day to see him. What we had in common was bigger than our differences. I saw him as a man who

Dot Day and Barbara Gaddy

loved his family and worked hard to provide for them. I saw him as the person everybody trusted and came to. To be truthful, he was the first person that I saw that I thought, "He is exactly what God intended when He created Him." He was not perfect. He did not do the work that you or I may think ethical, but his heart drew me in. I found out several months later that Kat was a big man in the neighborhood. I found out that he put the word out to everyone that they needed to shop with me, but they could not rob me or take anything from that property. When someone broke in four months later, they only took the cash register that had $50 in it. Nothing else was touched or taken. That afternoon when I got there, Kat wanted to see the tape so he could take care of it. I thanked him and told him that we were fine, and all was well. Kat was miracle number four. He is a miracle and my friend for life. I will always be there for him the way he has been there for me.

Robert is always present in the neighborhood. He drives a big gold truck with a Kansas City Chiefs logo on the back window. Like clockwork, Robert arrives around 10:30 a.m. and sits across the street next to the store with his truck backed in. He gets a small bottle of liquor and is there for the day. I can count on Robert to be there. He will always have a partner in the truck, and they will just chill. People come up and talk all through the day. Robert is unique in that he does not always color inside the lines. He is dependable but sometimes he will surprise. On Valentine's Day he brought me chocolate candy and a teddy bear. I am certain he did not have the money for that, but that is Robert. He often would bring me fruits or vegetables that he picked up at the local foodbank. He is just what you would call a good fellow. His truck has dents in a number of places, but his heart is kind and whole. We hit it off and once daily he would ride through, not wanting anything but leaving with a cookie. Robert is my miracle number five. You may see Robert and think he is just an old drunk, but I see him as steady and

Battles: Glimpses of Truth

faithful and just Robert. I see that he is exactly what God intended when he created him.

Cam works at the laundry mat next door to the bakery. Early on I let Cam and his mom know that we would just be neighbors taking care of each other. We would never exchange money. He would watch out for me and keep the lot clean, and I would look after him. Best deal I ever made in my life. His mom moved on to another location to work but often calls me just to check in. Cam and I worked there every day. He is a grown man with a childlike innocence. It is beautiful until someone takes advantage of him. He is a lamb among lions. I pray for him every day that nobody hurts Cam. I wish you could meet him. He would do anything for anybody if you ask of him. He loves shaved ice. That began our connection. He is over six feet and stocky. You would feel safe in my neighborhood with Cam by your side. I selfishly put Cam on my family plan and gave him a phone just so I could reach him. He has become my big little brother and one of those people that God sees as prince among men. God looks at his life as an act of praise and worship. He taught me that if I am ever going to be great, my heart must remain like a little child. This miracle number six is the greatest and rarest of all treasures.

French is a man among men. He is a beautiful father to his daughter. They came one Sunday. French owns the Bar B Que shack right down the street. People look to him when they are in need, and I have never seen him turn anyone away. At Christmas, he takes his whole operation to the park and feeds the homeless. I committed to joining him this year with cookies and cupcakes. Not too long ago a young girl who was in and out of homelessness was found dead from an overdose. I did not know her name, but I saw her from time to time. French invited everyone to his shop and did a celebration of life in honor and memory of her. He taught me so much about business, but the greatest lesson he taught me was that every life mattered. Every life has value, and none in our

Dot Day and Barbara Gaddy

neighborhood would go uncelebrated. I promise you two hundred people showed up for the celebration. They sang, they danced, they ate, and they honored life. Prior to this, I did not celebrate every life that way. I previously put others down to lift myself up. I rode past people with signs as if they were not there. I pray I never forget how it feels to miss an opportunity to return someone to themselves and remind them that every life matters. French is miracle number seven.

Precious was the first person I have ever met that loved the streets. You could find Precious walking somewhere day or night. Even though she is thirty, her mom looks after her and keeps a roof over her head, but she does not stay there. She would rather be in the street. Everybody knows her and everyone likes her. She can always produce a dollar for a Pina Colada shaved ice. Precious has children in the system that she goes every Sunday morning to church to see. She does not have a car, license, or the ability to get there, but she finds a way. She will tell me she loves me every time she leaves the building. Precious has more outstanding warrants than anybody I will ever meet.

Last month Precious was in jail for a week. When she came out, she did not change a thing. She loves the streets. She is the biggest defender of the homeless. She knows them all; she can tell you their stories. She is street savvy but often you can tell her heart is searching. Her name is Precious, and she is just that. Not what you and I may consider the definition, but I suspect exactly God's definition. I cannot reach her to restore her to herself. I cannot change her and would not really want to. In all my life, I wondered how God saw me. I suspect it is the same way I see Precious in all her imperfections and baggage, and yet I am drawn to her. I cannot change her and even if I could, I would not, given that her life is an act of worship. I find myself standing in awe of what she has to carry, rather than in judgement of how she carries it. Precious is miracle number eight.

Battles: Glimpses of Truth

Young Gun works nights at the Nissan Plant. On weekends he and his buds would come by. They had semi-automatic rifles on the seat and would greet me at the window with "Hey, Mama." They would eat brownies and drink hot chocolate. They would stay a while at the window if there was no one behind them. I would thank them for coming by and tell them to be safe out there. They would laugh, and off they would go. I keep a picture of them at my desk at home from the security camera of the three of them with guns hanging out of their belts sitting on the bakery porch. I pray that they will live long enough to realize their own potential. These beautiful souls are miracle number nine, ten and eleven.

I could keep writing page after page of the miracles of creation I met. I could share with you their stories one by one. In all my experiences, I can tell you that I have yet to meet a neighbor that did not change me for the better. I smile wider now when I see a father with his daughters. After twenty years of existing here, I now belong. I do not run in fear when something has happened in my neighborhood now. It activates my heart to respond. I know people by their name and by vehicle. It is not where I live now. It is where I belong. I am living proof that we do not go to the margins to change others; we go there so that we can be changed.

Due to circumstances at work, I had to close the bakery because I could not be there to manage it. The building is doing even greater work as a kitchen for the local church. The service to the community will continue, and they often let me come participate. It just reminds me that our paths are not always what we envisioned, but every act has a purpose for the future. The riches I gained from this experience and the friends I met are priceless. I could not be more grateful for my neighbors and my neighborhood and the safety and blessing I feel. I can only pray that you have an opportunity in life to experience something similar that leads you home. No matter where you call home, it is the greatest miracle of all. You are what God intended when He created you.

MEMORIAL DAY WITH GRANNY

Jas Clark

As I am looking out this window of life, I remember a special Memorial Day with Granny.

Granny told me to get up early one morning – "We have some things to do. It's Memorial Day."

She told me she was going to teach me about honor that day. "We are going to make flower bouquets and give honor where honor is due. We are honoring our soldiers who died to keep us free, giving honor to those brave soldiers who didn't make it home alive."

Granny grew flowers of all kinds, but that day she gathered her red, white, and blue flowers. She was making little bouquets tied up with red, white, and blue ribbons and asked me to help. In the spring every year, my Granny's yard was an explosion of color everywhere from her flowers. I asked, "What are we doing?"

She answered, "I told you – I'm going to teach you about honor today. Honor actually came from Bible times," she told me. "They would weigh their coins, and the more they weighed the more they were worth. The greater the value we put on the Lord, people, and things, the more those things are valued by us – and we will

Dot Day and Barbara Gaddy

be influenced by that throughout our lives." Granny told me that I should put the Lord as the very first thing I value, because He should be my biggest influence in my life.

My mama drove up to pick us up and Granny told me that we were going to the cemetery, to honor our soldiers who died while fighting for us in all the wars. "We have a list of names. I wish I could do this on every grave in America, but I can't do them all, because there are so many."

We left to go to a few cemeteries where we placed flowers on the graves of soldiers who died in the wars. I felt every grave should get some, but Granny explained, "We are only honoring our fallen soldiers today."

There was one grave where, as I bent down to put his flowers in the vase, I saw his photo on his tombstone. I'll never forget his face. He was so good looking and so very young. I told Granny, "He is so handsome – my goodness – and so young. This is so sad."

She said, "I wish every one had a photo so people could see how young they really were. They had their whole lives ahead of them."

My Granny stood at the gate looking across the cemetery, and even though there were only a few that had flowers, they stood out with honor. Granny said, "They are now honored and decorated for taking their last breath to protect our American soil for all of us. My sweet child, this is what honor looks like."

I told my mama and Granny, "I bet their families are so sad today. We should have gotten them flowers too."

Then Granny smiled as she replied, "My sweet child, your mama is going to take us for a visit – we have one more delivery." We drove up to a beautiful house, and a lady I had never met walked out on the porch. She was so delighted when she saw my Granny, and hugged and hugged mama and Granny – and even hugged me.

Battles: Glimpses of Truth

"We have a special delivery for you," Granny told her. I pulled out the last bouquet of flowers from behind my back, and the sweet lady cried and cried.

She told mama and Granny she was honored they thought of her. "It's a hard weekend, being Memorial Day. But I'm proud of my boy. He gave his life for freedom. Some don't appreciate it, but y'all do – and that melts my heart."

The sweet lady gave us cake and lemonade and we all talked as she showed us pictures of her son. I felt like this was what honor looked like, because her heart seemed to have been broken for a long time – but she was so proud of her son.

Granny told her that she was going to honor her in prayer. "We can honor you by covering you in prayer on such a painful day." Then Granny prayed this prayer, "Dear Heavenly Father, let us give honor where honor is due. Let us all call out the good in others' lives. Let us all be faithful in covering others in prayer. Let us keep our military safe, and pray for the ones who have sorrow from losing a loved one fighting for us to stay free. We honor each of them today, Lord. In Jesus' Heavenly Name, Amen."

We left and I asked Granny, "Do you know all those soldiers in the cemetery where we put flowers?"

She answered, "No, baby girl, I don't know them. But, in my heart, I feel I owe them for how they died for all of us to live free in America."

"Granny," I said, "they are probably all in Heaven, and they would be proud we put flowers on their graves."

Granny responded, "That is true. But tonight we thank them, because we are free to pray. I feel honored that I was able to do what we did today."

I know Memorial Day is celebrated with cookouts, big store sales, fun in the sun, and the beginning of summer. It is an awesome day to have a celebration – but just think of the moms and

Dot Day and Barbara Gaddy

dads that never saw their child again, or wives who grieved and only had memories and photos for their children to see.

On Memorial Day, please – in your moments of celebration – remember them and say a prayer for the families of those who gave their lives, and thank them for your freedom. The day my Granny decided to teach me about honor is a day I won't forget.

I feel like it should be called *Honor Day*.

That day with Granny was a real Memorial Day for me – and one I will never forget.

Let us remember to keep our military in our prayers at all times, giving thanks for the soldiers, being thankful that we can pray at any time, and expressing gratitude that we get to worship the Lord freely.

"We give thanks to God always for you all, making mention of you in our prayers." 1 Thessalonians 1:2

TWO FREDS – 2023

Fred Crans

Every year at this time I think of what has happened in my life as well as what didn't happen for 58,000 other Americans and 2,000,000 Vietnamese because of the Vietnam war. Politics aside, over 2,000,000 people perished in that war and never got to enjoy the long life I have been blessed with. This post, an annual remembrance, calls attention to one young man I knew well.

On May 1, 1995, I wrote:

April 30, 1995, marked the twentieth anniversary of the United States' withdrawal from Vietnam. It is a date that seems to have become destined for routine remembrance and recall by those of us who lived through the era – one that can seldom be revisited without tears.

As I sat at home yesterday watching the commemorative programs, I could not help but think about the story of the Two Freds. Fred Crans and Fred Fedder graduated from Haverling Central School in Bath, New York; Crans in 1963 and Fedder a year before, in 1962. After high school, both attended Corning Community College for two years. Fred Crans was an unfocused young man who distinguished himself by flunking out, while Fred Fedder, more confident and focused, completed his studies. Both eventually

Dot Day and Barbara Gaddy

joined the military – Crans becoming a hospital corpsman serving with the Marines, and Fedder a Warrant Officer helicopter pilot with the Army.

Fred Crans came back on a MedEvac flight after finishing his tour. Fred Fedder came back differently. His name is inscribed on The Wall. Fred Crans is approaching fifty. Fred Fedder is forever twenty-three.

Whenever I think about Vietnam these days, it is seldom about what was "right or wrong," but about the horrendous and senseless waste of lives. Also, it is often about how so many of us go through this life cursing our fate, never once taking a moment to appreciate the good that is present in every moment we are afforded.

Fred Fedder never got a chance to carve out a life. Fred Crans got the chance to start over. He went to the University of Miami, where he graduated with honors. He got married, started a family, got divorced, picked up a Master's Degree, got married and divorced a second time, and still had the blessings of another chance. Many would look at Fred Crans' life and say that he was a failure, considering all the opportunities he had been given. Others might think that his was representative of life among the Baby Boomers – a constant series of actions, effects, rebounds, and so on, ad mortis.

From an outsider's perspective, any of those observations would be correct. Fred Crans currently lives in a two-bedroom apartment in Waterloo, Iowa. His children live in Canton, Ohio, with his first wife. He is starting over one more time. Like so many others who have encountered the downside of life, he has experienced depression first-hand. At times he has thought about running away to live a hermit's life in Mexico.

Or worse.

But whenever he has been faced with that gloom and possible doom, two things have always brought him back: the thought of the terrible price his children would have to pay for such a stupid

Battles: Glimpses of Truth

and capricious act, and the thought of his high school and college friend, Fred Fedder, who never got the second, third, fourth and fifth chances at life that he was given.

Maybe on every April 30th, the best use any of us Vietnam-era human beings can make of the time is this: Think of the 58,000 plus people whose names inscribed on The Wall represent lives never fully lived. We cannot bring them back. We can make a pledge not to let future generations suffer death in such a cavalier and meaningless fashion. And we can decide to find meaning and value in both the successes and failures that are part of the everyday lives that those 58,000 plus human souls were denied.

Take care, Freddy, I miss you.

Fred

2014 Update

In the nineteen years since I wrote those words, my personal life has continued to take its meandering course. Soon after I wrote the tribute, I got custody of my youngest son, and two years later I was living in Ohio again with both my boys. My life seemed to be a constantly improving scenario, with personal and professional success abounding.

Today, I am married for the third time and living in Dubuque, Iowa with my wonderful wife Cathy, my two dogs, Buddy and Rhea, and my cat, Kianna. My sons live in St. Louis and Nashville and I have two wonderful grandchildren.

During those same eighteen years, we have proved that the lessons of Vietnam were short-lived at best, and another 4,000+ Americans and hundreds of thousands of Iraqis and Afghans have paid with their lives needlessly and without justification.

Every Memorial Day, I think of my friend, Fred Fedder – what a great guy he was – always friendly and engaging, even to outsiders like myself. I think about how neither he nor the 58,000 plus other Americans (and the hundreds of thousands of Vietnamese) who were killed in that conflict deserved to have their lives erased over political hegemony.

And every year – at least for one part of one day – I know how fortunate I am.

Author's note: Since my last revision, Buddy died, Rhea died, Kianna died and my marriage died. I have moved back to Cleveland where I live in a little house with my best friend Dusty, a red tick coonhound.

2019 Update

Time rolls on. I'm still in Cleveland and I have added another coonhound, Isabelle (Izzy) and a calico cat, Ginger to the squad. I work part time and coach Little League. I try to not be overwhelmed by my disappointment in the supposed leader of this country, but in the words of Johnny Cash, "I Press On," with the knowledge that ensuing generations will solve the problems my generation and its greed created.

All of those of us who served in combat understand the finality of death at a young age. Those who honor those of us who served, no matter how sincere their sentiments, cannot possibly understand the context of war. Those who lost loved ones mourn a lifetime for the sons, daughters, grandsons, and granddaughters they have been denied.

2021 Update

Last year was truly terrible – between the pandemic that has killed nearly 600,000 people, the political unrest, racial violence, and the insurrection against the U.S. Capitol, we have had a lot to digest. Over the course of the past four years, I have lost many friends – some to death and others to political differences. No matter how they were lost, the effect is an unhappy one. Still, I am here – soldiering on.

Battles: Glimpses of Truth

I try to remember this: On the worst day of my life, I am still alive and have an opportunity to enjoy the beauty of this world – something that was denied to my friend Fred Fedder and thousands of others like him.

Take care, pal. I'll stop by the next time I'm in Washington.

2022 Update

This year – another reason to pause and reflect. Much is written about those who "died for our freedom" – a phrase that is well-intentioned, but generally covers up a significant number of false truths. The only war in the last one hundred years that approached being a threat to our freedom was WWII. The rest have all been contrived for politics or profit or both. When I was a corpsman serving with the Marines in Vietnam, I never heard anyone say, "I'm here to die for my fellow Americans' freedom." Every single person began counting the number of days until his rotation back to CONUS (Continental United States) the second their boots touched the ground. Few to none ever joined the military to chase glory. I joined after flunking out of college. The service was going to be my second chance. When people who don't know me say the banal, "Thank you for your service," I shake it off. What do they know about how and why I served?

I certainly didn't serve so that idiots could buy the same weapons that we used in Vietnam to hunt defenseless deer or other similarly-defenseless human beings. Freddy Fedder didn't die for the Second Amendment. He didn't die so that second, third and fourth graders could be ambushed and wiped out in their classrooms. Truth is, Freddy Fedder and the 58,000-plus other Americans did not die for altruism. Rather, they died to help the high rollers of the military/industrial complex achieve their goals of attaining fabulous wealth at the expense of those less fortunate and less connected.

Dot Day and Barbara Gaddy

To those in power, Freddy Fedder was just a meaningless statistic.

The same is true of the most recent 21 victims of the mass shooting in Uvalde, Texas. Kids just going to school and a sicko with access to assault rifles ends their lives. Amidst the furor and the inevitable call from the "snowflakes" to enact gun control legislation, the Second Amendment freaks will demand that either nothing be done, or that EVERYBODY be armed. After a couple of weeks, the 21 deaths will fade into the woodwork, and idiots will be able to buy weapons of mass destruction before they can legally drink and their fathers and uncles (inevitably angry white men) will be able to build their designer deer stands, replete with color television sets, heaters, running water and bunk beds, and shoot defenseless herbivores (with those same assault rifles) who are just trying to get enough nourishment to make it through the winter, then go home and regale their families with stories of their exploits as fearless "hunters," all while tearing up when the National Anthem is being played and thanking ex-military members for their service.

There is a big difference between the Bambi's, the innocent school kids and teachers, and the Fred Fedders of the world. Deer and little kids are truly unsuspecting and defenseless victims of something they have (or had) no idea of what is about to happen. Freddy Fedder, on the other hand, knew what he was doing when he enlisted, as did I.

Maybe at least for a day, we should remember those who were innocent victims of mass shootings, the innocent Vietnamese we killed, and who knows how many other victims of corporate greed and indifference.

If Freddy Fedder died protecting our freedom, then the innocent animals and children that continue to be killed in the name of "our rights" are nothing but victims of those freedoms.

Battles: Glimpses of Truth

I'm sorry Freddy. You didn't die for this. Your life deserves a better legacy. You were a great guy – better than many of the people whose freedoms you were allegedly defending.

Rest easy, brother. I, for one, will keep speaking out.

WAR EFFORT

Lottie Brent Boggan

"Miss Langley."

Sally Fran jumped when the teacher called her name, her face flushed, as if she were on fire. She sucked in a deep breath and dropped her head.

"Well?" Her teacher lifted a brow. "Are you buying any?"

"No, ma'am," Sally Fran answered, although the three dimes weighed heavily in her pocket. She needed them on Saturday for her treat.

The teacher dipped her chin, looked over glasses as if she knew something Sally Fran didn't, and then she went on to the next name.

Frightened the coins might roll out, Sally Fran stuck her hand into her skirt to make sure they were still there. She jerked her hand from her pocket; the hot dimes had seared her fingertips.

Most children saved dimes all week long to buy Savings Stamps. Shoulders back, their chests filled with pride, every Friday they walked up the aisle with their money. Sally Fran had chosen to skip this week's procession to the teacher's desk.

That night when she crawled into bed, a twinge of conscience kept her awake later than usual. If her mother or daddy ever learned she still had her dimes, it would be Katy-bar-the-door. She was safe enough, though. They would never find out. Right?

Dot Day and Barbara Gaddy

The lights were off, the blackout curtains drawn, and yet she still couldn't drop off to sleep. She imagined Jesus standing at the foot of her bed. She couldn't hide from Jesus. He knew what she had done. When she was a bad girl, Jesus wept.

When Sally Fran woke up Saturday morning, she had forgotten all about making Jesus cry. She was worried the devil might have sneaked in during the night; he might have snatched the coins so he could give her money to the Germans or the Japs. The first thing she did was check and make sure the dimes were still under her pillow.

The dimes were there.

Brother rolled over in bed, looked at her, and sucked his thumb.

Concerned with buying herself a treat and forgetting she had stolen from the war effort with her act of treason, all morning she thought only about the ice cream she could buy later in the day. Should she have chocolate, peach, or vanilla?

That afternoon, while her mother picked beans in their Victory Garden, Sally Fran ran to the kitchen. She slipped their War Ration Book in her pocket, got on her bike and pedaled down to Carr's Grocery Store. Mr. Carr still filled call-in-orders for his customers. Luckily for her, however, no other customers were in the store waiting for him to fill their grocery orders, so she could walk right up to the glass display case.

Sally Fran stood staring at the small buckets of ice cream behind the glass for so long, the usually patient Mr. Carr finally said, "Go ahead and make up your mind, little lady. I've got orders to fill."

She pressed her nose against the cold glass counter, fogging it up, and slowly pointed toward the vanilla. A few minutes later, gripping her ice cream cone in one hand, she steered her bike with the other. She managed to take a few licks of the creamy custard while she rode, but the gravel street was bumpy, and she smeared the tacky sweet across her face.

Battles: Glimpses of Truth

At the hairpin curve leading from Rolling Meadows to Champion Hill Heights, she backpedaled to put on the brakes. All week long she had thought about enjoying this sweet treat but the ice cream cone really didn't taste very good. On this day she had succumbed to deception and greed to buy it. She had made Jesus cry.

Steering her bike onto the edge of the road, she planted both feet on the ground and rubbed her nose and cheeks on the shoulder of her bright blue sunsuit. The ice cream was still on her face. Almost ready to cry, she put her weight on her right leg, popped down the kick stand with her left, and wiped more of the sticky, sugary cream off with her hand.

The rumble of an airplane propeller over toward the air base caught Sally Fran's attention. She hopped off her bike, held her ice cream cone and the handlebars with one hand so she could shield her eyes and look toward the steely gray sky. Her eyes stung and watered. Although she couldn't see the plane, "Off we go, into the wild blue yonder," she sang, then bent over and took another lick.

With a sigh, she raised her head. The creamy taste of vanilla had burned her mouth and made her feel as if she were choking, not on ice cream but on a mouthful of salty ocean water. What was left of the tilted custard slid off the cone and onto the gravel road. She stared down at it, but for some reason, losing the treat didn't seem to matter much anymore.

She swiped the back of her hand across her mouth, then licked off the sticky smear. She climbed back on her bike, hurriedly rode home, and slipped in the back door.

"Sister, finish bathing Brother," her mother called from the kitchen.

Sally Fran's baby brother was in the bathroom splashing water. He had a toy German submarine in one hand, and an American sub in the other.

Dot Day and Barbara Gaddy

"Hudn, hudn, hudn," he chanted as he moved them through the water.

"Hurry up," Sally Fran fussed.

"You didn't buy your war stamps, you didn't buy your war stamps," he said in a singsong voice. "I'm gonna tell. I'm gonna tell."

"Shut up! I'll tell Mama you pulled Lula May's pants down and peed in the front yard."

"I didn't do neither one," he whined indignantly.

Sally Fran didn't really know whether he had or not. He looked guilty, and since he was just five years old, he had probably done both things, or maybe even something much worse.

She went into mother's bedroom, sank down in her soft chintz chair, and tugged the brass pull cord on the floor lamp. She picked up a *Life Magazine*, twisted a lock of blond hair around her fingers, and slowly turned the pages.

A full-page black and white drawing of a young pilot filled the back cover. Streaks of light spilling through the woven lampshade scattered gold, starry patches across his face. He stood on the wing of his plane. Waves lapped over the wing as the plane sank into the ocean, while evil black triangles circled round him.

Sharks!

The pilot stretched up onto his toes as far as he could. A sad smile on his face, he had one hand on the cockpit and saluted with the other hand, as he looked toward the heavens.

He died for you! Did you buy your U.S. Savings Stamps this week?

Bitter tears streaked down Sally Fran's gummy cheeks, and she ran into the bathroom.

"Quit playing, Brother," she screamed at him. "Look what I did!"

"What?" Her brother didn't look up. "Hudn, hudn, hudn."

Battles: Glimpses of Truth

"He died. I killed him," Sally Fran whispered. She held the picture in front of Brother so he could see how wicked his big sister was for letting the pilot die. "I'm so bad. He drowned. The sharks ate him. Because I didn't buy war stamps."

"Hudn, hudn, hudn." With a submarine in each hand, her brother headed them on a collision course.

"Don't you see?" She begged him to understand what she felt about letting one of their brave soldiers die.

He paid her no attention, so she raised her chin and looked heavenward.

"Oh, Jesus. I am so sorry," she whispered. "I made you cry."

Baby brother took a deep breath and filled his cheeks with air. He flopped back under the water and blew out churning bubbles, much like the ones a sinking U-boat or thrashing sharks would make.

Water splashed over the rim of the tub onto the green linoleum floor.

Sally Fran wept. Her heartbeat came in surges, like the waves coiling to sweep over the doomed young pilot. Hot water strangled her throat. Still holding the magazine, she tried to raise the commode seat with her free hand but didn't quite make it. As she leaned over to retch into the toilet, a thin stream of vomit splashed across the pilot's picture.

"Kapow!" With a loud splash, her brother popped out of the water. "We win the war. I killed the Krauts!"

ABOUT THE AUTHORS

Barbara Grillot Gaddy is a native of Crystal Springs, Mississippi. She holds a Master of Education degree from Mississippi College, Clinton, Mississippi, and held teaching certifications in both business and computer education. She started the kindergarten program at First Baptist Church, Crystal Springs, where she directed the program and taught 2-year-old preschoolers. She wrote curriculum for the Southern Baptist Convention, with a focus on guidance for teachers of five-year-old children.

Barbara taught business and computer classes at high school and community college levels. She was recruited to begin the computer education program at Ingalls Shipbuilding, Pascagoula, Mississippi, and taught computer applications classes, network administration classes, and mainframe operations classes for Ingalls employees from the president of the company to the shop floor workers. During this time Barbara authored two instruction manuals for Microsoft Access Database Management, developing case studies and teaching instructions for college level instructors. She continued her career at Ingalls for twenty years, serving in positions of Information Technology Program Manager and Manager of Information Technology Communications.

She currently is a substitute teacher for a local school and volunteers her time reviewing and ranking applications for the Vietnam

Helicopter Pilot Association (VHPA) / Army Aviation Association of America (AAAA) scholarships.

Barbara and her husband Bruce, a Vietnam veteran, enjoy life on their 172-acre farm in Crystal Springs, where they fish, tend a fruit tree garden, ride four wheelers, and just enjoy life together. Barbara has three children and four grandchildren.

Dorothy Ainsworth Day believes if a bumblebee can fly when it is aerodynamically incapable of flight she can write when it is physically impossible to do nothing on her own. But even when she thinks she is doing the work, she has a tribe supporting her efforts. She has degrees from Copiah-Lincoln Community College, Wesson, Mississippi, and Mississippi College, Clinton, Mississippi; formerly she was a licensed teacher of high school English and French and a licensed marriage and family therapist.

She and her caregiver/husband Charles laugh at the cute antics of Dempsey, a miniature Aussie ($^1/_8$) Schnoodle ($^3/_8$ poodle, ½ Schnauzer), attend church, and roll through life together. They discuss their legacy writing, and plan together how to tell Lady's story. Lady was their Bitsa rescue from a shelter (bits of wolf, shepherd, collie, and more).

Although Dot wrote poetry or rhyming verses in the first grade, there is no proof it existed. She worked to get her students to enjoy the process of writing and later her four grandchildren to relish the processes of drawing and painting ("Benches, swings, table prepare you for owning a home or get you ready for a career!").

Dot had a variety of jobs, but her life was working for her family as wife, mother, mother-in-law, daughter, daughter-in-law, and as grandmother. Although she might have embarrassed family members sometimes, her over-arching goal was and is to love and honor Jesus.

Dot was sidelined from her careers and chaired from the independence of driving by IBM. Yes, IBM – Inclusion Body Myositis, a late-onset muscular dystrophy of unknown origin and no treatment. She looked to writing to live out her purposes. She accumulated the stories of others for her first published book, *Memories of a Sharecropper's Family.* Her second effort, aided by the formidable Barbara Gaddy, resulted in the retelling of ordinary events touched with the handprints of God – *Ordinary Miracles.* It was an anthology, as is *Battles: Glimpses of Truth*.

CONTRIBUTORS
Writers of Stories, Tellers of Tales, and Poets

Carol Ashley: "To John Upon His Return"
Carol Ashley is a retired schoolteacher and an attack poet. If she sees someone she thinks might benefit, she springs one of her humorous verses on him. She enjoys traveling, painting, writing short stories, and light verse. Her first book of poetry was **Growing Old Disgracefully**. *Her first novel is* **Shattered Jade**.

Lottie Brent Boggan: "The Twenty-Fourth of May" "Seventy-Five Years, Come and Gone" "War Effort"
Lottie Brent Boggan has a knack for finding humor in the worst of circumstances. She's been a long-time contributor to the Northside Sun, a weekly newspaper in Jackson, Mississippi. Lottie has had numerous accolades, winning The Eudora Welty novel competition, placing at the Faulkner Wisdom Competition, and receiving newspaper column awards. In addition to her novels, she has also compiled multiple anthologies of short stories and served as editor to several critically acclaimed authors besides herself. She was a founder of The Red Dog Writers and is a member of Middle Mississippi Chapter of the Mississippi Writers Guild, The Jackson Chapter of the Mississippi Writers Guild, and Mississippi Gulf Coast Writers Association.

Dot Day and Barbara Gaddy

*Lottie's family is somewhat of an icon in Mississippi, with her father having started Brent's Drugs, which was featured in the movie, **The Help**. Her late husband was a founder of River Oaks Hospital, now Merit.*

Gail Shows Bouldin: "Vagabond"

Gail has retired from her career as a nurse. She is now firmly planted in Kosciusko, Mississippi, with her husband of 20 years and is enjoying activities with her many friends.

David Ching: "A Tall Glass of Tell-It-Like-It-Is Juice"

Rev. David Ching lived with the knowledge of his impending death from cancer for several years; however, in his physical struggle, he demonstrated grace and strength that provided encouragement and positivity for all who knew him.

He was born April 23, 1965, in Hazlehurst, Mississippi. He grew up in Crystal Springs and was a graduate of Union Academy. After serving ten years in the United States Army and United States Air Force, he served as pastor in the Nazarene Church. For the past twelve years he pastored churches in Granby, Missouri, and Houston, Mississippi. He also served as a member of the Houston, Mississippi volunteer fire department. He graduated with a Bachelor's degree from Nazarene Bible College (Colorado Springs, Colorado) and went on to receive his Master of Divinity from Northwest Nazarene University (Nampa, Idaho).

David Ching passed away December 23, 2015.

Jasmin "Jas" Clark: "Memorial Day with Granny"

Jas Clark was born and reared on a country farm in Simpson County, Mississippi. She had her best loved ones teaching her about the Lord and trying to keep her off a colorful path. She lost each of them – her daddy, her mama, and especially her sweet granny. She retired from teaching school and then taught kindergarten. This got her ready for her next journey, taking care of her mother. After spending 10 years taking care of her mother with Alzheimer's, the Lord started giving her memories every morning from her loved ones in heaven. She states, "I feel life does not build by only positivity but also through the hardships. I guess folks call hardships negativity. Hardships teach you to appreciate the beautiful moments of your life and see how much the Lord blesses us. The Lord gave me a quote, 'I'm a sinner trying to do better.'"

Fred Crans: "Two Freds – 2023"
Fred Crans currently serves as healthcare business development executive for St. Onge company, a world recognized supply chain engineering and logistics consulting firm. He has decades of experience as a hospital supply chain leader. Fred is a frequent contributor to **Healthcare Purchasing News***. His blogs may be read on the LinkedIn website. Fred is a Vietnam survivor.*

Josh Dawson: "Cucumbers and Pickles – My Story of Battling PTSD"
Josh Dawson worked as a paramedic in Mississippi for seventeen years before moving on in June 2023 to become the program manager for the Mississippi Department of Health EMS Department. He is certified for both neonatal resuscitation-NRP-and the critical care transport service – CCEMTP. He and his wife Jessica live in central Mississippi.

Dot Day: "Coaching to Win "Bruce Gaddy: Death Dealer #22 – Nineteen Minutes to Live" "TopGun: Steve Spragg's Story" "Stoic Patriot Bill Day" "Naked on the Back Porch" "The Ground Forces" "Drought"
Dot Day retired entirely too young because of inclusion body myositis, a late onset muscular dystrophy. Her careers were in high school education, where she taught English and foreign languages,

Dot Day and Barbara Gaddy

and in family counseling. Dot's first book was a family history, **Memories of a Sharecroppers Family**. Her first anthology was **Ordinary Miracles**.

Barbara Gaddy "20/20 Determination" "Swimming Katrina – or Black Lace and Sandals" "Bruce Gaddy: Death Dealer #22 – Nineteen Minutes to Live" "Introverted Excellence" "Zeb, Gunner, and Kye" "From Boredom to Brilliance"
Barbara is a retired educator and communications manager. She earned her Master of Education degree with teaching certifications in Business and Computer Education from Mississippi College in Clinton, Mississippi, and taught at high school and community college levels. Barbara was recruited by Ingalls Shipbuilding in Pascagoula, Mississippi, to develop their Computer Education Program, instructing employees in software applications, networking administration, and mainframe data transfer. Her subsequent positions at Northrop Grumman/Ingalls Shipbuilding included Information Technology Program Manager for various Ingalls functional business units, as well as Manager of Information Technology Communications. She is married to Bruce Gaddy and has three grown children and four grandchildren.

Bruce Gaddy: "Bruce Gaddy: Death Dealer #22 – Nineteen Minutes to Live"
Bruce is a native of Crystal Springs Mississippi, where he has lived all his life, except for his time spent in Vietnam as an Army Helicopter Pilot. His military service is detailed in this book in the story, "Bruce Gaddy: Death Dealer #22 – Nineteen Minutes to Live." Bruce was awarded two Bronze Stars, The Distinguished Flying Cross, and 36 Air Medals representing over 900 hours of combat flying time. His diagnosis of service-connected diabetes soon after returning from Vietnam forced him to retire from flying helicopters at Hawkins Field in Jackson, Mississippi. He

Battles: Glimpses of Truth

subsequently worked at Kuhlman Electric/ABB in Crystal Springs Mississippi, and also worked in the field of seismography. Bruce and his wife Barbara, co-author of this book, live in his life-long home in Crystal Springs, Mississippi.

Gail Harvey-Walker: "I Am" "Black Water" "The Swordsman"
Gail is a native of Copiah County, Mississippi, born in 1966 at Hardy Wilson Memorial Hospital in Hazlehurst, Mississippi. Her particular disorder is arthrogryposis which causes bones to be fused at the joints. Any joint can be affected, but in her case, it is her knees. She also has a club foot, drooping eyelid, hip dysplasia, and a mild case of scoliosis. Gail spent the first few months of her life in a body cast, crying from daylight to dark.

Fortunately, she was born into a family who loves her unconditionally. She was also blessed with a huge independent streak and a (mostly) happy disposition. Gail doesn't pretend that her life has always been perfect, because she has many days when she wonders why she is here. However, over the years Gail has come to accept and love herself, and now tries to share some of her knowledge about life and love with others.

Lynn Bush King: "To My Son, Archie Ray Bush, Jr. – 1972-2009"
Lynn Bush King has recently become serious about her writing since her retirement from a baking career. She enjoys life in the country with her animals. Lynn's interests are her family, traveling, and her church – where "she's the one in the hat."

Patti Lamar: "Is God Good?"
Patti Lamar is a native of Crystal Springs, Mississippi, and is retired from her service as a Vocational Rehabilitation Counselor. She studied Rehabilitation Counseling at The University of Southern Mississippi, in Hattiesburg, Mississippi, and the University of Georgia in Athens, Georgia. Patti is an avid advocate for hospital

patients' rights following the 2022 death from Covid of her beloved husband Ray.

Philip Levin, MD: "Medical Missions"
Philip L. Levin, MD has worked as an emergency room doctor for over 40 years. He served as president of the Gulf Coast Writers Association for 12 years, where he promoted writers through the **Magnolia Quality Quarterly**. *He edited and wrote for eight anthologies. Philip's writing covers several age groups and genres: three children's photo books from his travels as a volunteer medical missionary, three chapter books for early readers, and a book for three-year-olds. He has written historical fiction, fantasy, contemporary, romance, and numerous short stories.*

Hazel R. James Lonie: "Commercials, TV & Old Age"
Hazel R. James Lonie states, "Writing is one of my favorite hobbies. My writing started about two years after my mother's death. This therapy allowed me to verbalize emotions I couldn't talk about and hide within my writing. I have been able to exact the gravity of situations and realize the humanness in others and myself. Retiring from Jackson Public Schools with twenty-eight years of service, I taught art and tutored math and reading. There are times when I miss the hustle and bustle of teaching. Then I come to my senses and realize I'm not able to meet the demands of a full-time job."

Cindy Mount: "Awakening to God's Love" "I Have Met the Enemy"
Cindy Mount is a writer from Zachary, Louisiana, who loves God and shares her life through writing devotions that reflect God's love and grace. Her Christian testimony is to share the transforming work of God in her life. She has cultivated a strong, spiritual foundation rooted in scripture, and in her relationship with God as

she experiences difficult seasons in life. She also enjoys spending time with her husband of 43 years, family, and four pets.

Dr Bob Rich: "Maudie"
Dr. Bob Rich, Ph.D. earned his doctorate in psychology in 1972. He worked as an academic researcher and applied scientist until retiring the first time at 36 years of age. Later, he returned to psychology and qualified as a Counseling Psychologist, running a private practice for over 20 years. During this time, he was on the national executive board of the College of Counselling Psychologists of the Australian Psychological Society (APS), then spent three years as a Director of the APS. He was the therapist to whom referrers sent their most difficult cases. Bob retired in 2013, but still does pro bono counseling over the internet. This has given him hundreds of children and grandchildren he has never met, because many of these people stay in touch for years. His major joy in life is to be of benefit to others, which is why he wrote a book that's in effect a course of therapy. He has been an environmental activist since 1972, because he had young children and wanted a good future for them. Now, he has grandchildren and great-grandchildren and works for at least some chance of survival for them. He has authored 19 books.

Pauline Rule: "Sweet Relief"
Pauline Rule is the Chief of Staff, Compliance and Integrity Operations at AT&T Integrity Operations in Jackson, Mississippi. Her past roads led her from acquisitions agent, 1st level call center manager, performance development coach, area manager to her current position. She notes two pieces of memorable advice: "Never forget what it was like to take your first call," and "Be yourself – you are good enough." She uses her position to influence others to own the mission of living the company's four culture pillars. She works toward creating leaders. She earned a Master's

Dot Day and Barbara Gaddy

degree from Claremont Lincoln University. Within the past year she lost eighty pounds by riding a bike!

Janet Taylor-Perry: "Nothing in Life Is Free"
Janet Taylor-Perry, like many of her characters, is a history buff and loves anything of historical significance from old cars to old cemeteries. She has been critically acclaimed at the Faulkner Wisdom Competition; her writing continues to receive 4- and 5-star reviews. Readers can see so much of her in her characters: mother, educator, author, editor, and a person who has overcome great obstacles and still holds on to her faith.

Hardin M Wright: "War Diary of Staff Sgt. Hardin M. Wright"
Hardin M. Wright recorded his experiences as a POW in Germany on scraps and bits of paper. This story provides a record of his wartime experiences. Family members, Debbie Wright Webb and her daughter Jill Hoda, made this story available. After the war, he and his brother Romuel became entrepreneurs in Crystal Springs, Mississippi.

Printed in the USA
CPSIA information can be obtained
at www.ICGtesting.com
CBHW071323050724
11157CB00003B/16